Legal Theory Tod:
Evaluation and Legal

Legal Theory Today

General Editor of the Series

John Gardner, Professor of Jurisprudence, University of Oxford

TITLES IN THIS SERIES

Forthcoming titles:

Evaluation and Legal Theory

Julie Dickson

General Editor: Professor John Gardner

·HART·
PUBLISHING

OXFORD – PORTLAND OREGON
2001

Hart Publishing
Oxford and Portland, Oregon

Published in North America (US and Canada) by
Hart Publishing c/o
International Specialized Book Services
5804 NE Hassalo Street
Portland, Oregon
97213-3644
USA

Distributed in the Netherlands, Belgium and
Luxembourg by
Intersentia, Churchillaan 108
B2900 Schoten
Antwerpen
Belgium

Hart Publishing is a specialist legal publisher based in Oxford, England.
To order further copies of this book or to request a list of other
publications please write to:

Hart Publishing, Salter's Boatyard, Folly Bridge,
Abingdon Road, Oxford OX1 4LB
Telephone: +44 (0)1865 245533 or Fax: +44 (0)1865 794882
e-mail: mail@hartpub.co.uk
WEBSITE: http//www.hartpub.co.uk

British Library Cataloguing in Publication Data
Data Available
ISBN 1–84113–184–9 (hardback)
1–84113–081–8 (paperback)

Typeset by Hope Services (Abingdon) Ltd.
Printed and bound in Great Britain on acid-free paper by
Biddles Ltd, www.biddles.co.uk

General Editor's Preface

Legal philosophers have lately become ever more preoccupied with questions, not so much about law, as about legal philosophy itself. To what extent is legal philosophy objective? To what extent is it value free? To what extent is it descriptive? And so on. If one always suspected that the philosophy of law is a self-indulgent pursuit—and I have heard many lawyers and law students express that view with great vigour—then this recent growth industry (the philosophy of the philosophy of law, or meta-jurisprudence, as one might call it) may strike one as positively narcissistic. But in a way the anti-philosophical stance of many lawyers and law students is the very thing that explains the growth of this industry. When studying law one learns to demand an authority for every proposition. This demand tends to instill in the law student, and later in the lawyer, a sceptical attitude to all questions that cannot in principle be settled by authority. So the most far-fetched and incoherent forms of scepticism—forms that even the most sceptical literary theorists would find embarrassing—often take particularly deep root in the legal community. In some law schools there is almost an arms race to see who can out-sceptic their colleagues. It is perfectly understandable, against this backdrop, that those with a genuinely philosophical interest in law should gradually be drawn into ever more navel-gazing debate about the status of their own work as philosophers.

In this third book in the *Legal Theory Today* series, Julie Dickson avoids the navel-gazing and cuts through the existing meta-jurisprudential debate. To do so, she focuses specifically on the place of *evaluation* in legal philosophy. Many sceptics have talked as if the presence of evaluative elements in philosophical writings about law were somehow a dirty little secret. Legal philosophers who purported only to explain the nature of law in fact imported their own ideological predilections and inevitably ended up displaying the law in a favourable (or unfavourable) light. Nothing in legal philosophy was ever value-neutral, the allegation goes. Everything was either a secret defence or a secret critique of law. This allegation was designed to face legal philosophers with a dilemma. On the one hand, they could agree that their work on the nature of law actually constituted a defence (or critique) of law. On the other hand they could insist that all they were doing was 'describing' law, with their evaluative faculties switched off. The first option was thought to be unpalatable to most philosophers of law, while the second was thought to be incredible.

Many students have been taught to read the later phases of the debate between Dworkin and Hart as representing the struggle between the two horns of this dilemma. And many have concluded—as well one might—that the palating of the unpalatable has more going for it than the creding of the incredible. Hence they awarded victory to Dworkin, who (it is said) at least had the courage to admit that he was being ideo-logical, as surely the sceptics were right to say that all writers on law must be.

Julie Dickson beautifully destablilises this familiar student conclusion not by seizing the opposite horn of the dilemma but by showing that the dilemma was always an illusion. That legal philosophers must approach law evaluatively in order to explain its nature does not entail that every act of explaining the nature of law is an act of defending (or criticising) law. As Dickson puts it, there are 'indirect' as well as 'direct' roles for evaluation in legal philosophy. Even 'describing' law in the way that Hart wanted to do is an indirectly evaluative activity. But it does not follow that it conceals a defence (or critique) of law and so has a dirty little secret of the kind that the sceptics allege. Hart's method picks out what is *significant* about law—*and that itself is an evaluation*—but it leaves open whether what is significant about law is significantly good (as Dworkin claims it must be) or significantly bad (as an anarchist might claim in response). Here we have a kind of evaluation that does not decide between defence and critique and is, *in that limited dimension*, value-neutral. It leaves open whether one should be an anarchist or a law-lover, or indeed (like most of us) someone in between. But it does not involve switching off one's evaluative faculties and looking at one's subject through totally undiscriminating eyes, for that would indeed be incredible as a philosophical method —or indeed as any kind of intellectual approach.

The book sets itself modest ambitions. It aims to make logical space for "indirectly evaluative" legal theory without defending it as the right way to go. I tend to think that the book exceeds this ambition and brings out much that is attractive about the kind of legal theory that Dickson has in mind. More importantly, however, I like to think that the book may help to bring to an end the excessive polarisation on the subject of methodology that has marked the period since the publication of Dworkin's *Law's Empire*. Since *Law's Empire* appeared, the question is often raised, in Dworkinian terms, of whether one is an "interpretivist" concerning the nature of law. But everyone is an interpretivist concerning the nature of law and always has been. The works of Bentham, Kelsen and Hart were all of them equally interpretations of law and legally related phenomena. They all aimed to explain law and legally related phenomena in a way that played up the important and played down the unimportant. So the real issue is not whether we philosophers of law are necessarily interpreters; it is whether we are forced, as Dworkin thinks we are, to be *constructive* interpreters, i.e. to explain law in a way that shows it *favourably*, aligning the important with the importantly *good*. If Dickson is right—and I think she is—we need not be constructive interpreters. We can approach the problem of the nature of law as an evaluative problem, but still with a more open mind about law's value.

John Gardner
University College, Oxford
2 April 2001

Contents

Acknowledgements

First of all, I would like to thank Richard Hart and John Gardner for giving me the opportunity to write for the Legal Theory Today Series. I share their hopes that the series will both express and encourage a spirit of innovative inquiry within a flourishing discipline. John Gardner was a source of unobtrusive guidance and support at every stage of this project, which helped enormously in its completion. I am also grateful to all those at Hart Publishing for their careful attention in preparing the book for publication.

I received a great deal of assistance while I was developing the ideas expressed in this work. I am especially grateful to Joseph Raz for all of his guidance and encouragement, and I would particularly like to thank him for his advice in formulating the material which appears in Chapter 3 of the book. I also presented some of the ideas in this work to various audiences and discussion groups and would like to thank those who participated in a seminar in the Jurisprudence and Social Policy Program at the University of California at Berkeley in February 1998, in the Jurisprudence Discussion Group which met in Oxford in Trinity Term 1998, and in a staff seminar held in the Law Department of the University of Hull in November 1999 for their helpful comments and criticism. In addition to this, for discussions regarding and/or comments upon earlier versions of parts of the book, I am grateful to Elspeth Attwooll, Thérèse Björkholm, Yuri Borgmann-Prebil, John Gardner, Steve Gough, Aileen Kavanagh, Dori Kimel and Neil MacCormick. All remaining errors and imprecisions of expression are of course all my own work.

I would like to thank the Law Departments of the University of Leicester and of University College London for their support while I was completing this project. Thanks are due to many of

Acknowledgements

my colleagues at those institutions, and in the jurisprudential community in general, for their interest in the book, and for their collegiality, and I am particularly grateful to Malcolm Ross and Stephen Guest for all their encouragement. Last and most certainly not least, very special thanks are due to my friends and family, and especially to my mother, Janet Dickson, for their much appreciated support, patience and good humour.

Julie Dickson
University College London, November 2000

1
What's the Point of Jurisprudence?

Agathon: But it was you who proved that death doesn't exist.
Allen: Hey, listen—I've proved a lot of things. That's how I pay my rent. Theories and little observations. A puckish remark now and then. Occasional maxims. It beats picking olives, but let's not get carried away.
Agathon: But you have proved many times that the soul is immortal.
Allen: And it is! On paper. See, that's the thing about philosophy— it's not all that functional once you get out of class.[1]

Woody Allen.

A. Introduction: Outlining the Project

What's the point of jurisprudence? This question is, I suspect, likely to be on a lot of law students' minds upon first encountering the philosophical study of law. Although cynical and pejorative answers to it can easily be given, taken seriously, the question is an important one, because it invites us to explore some of the deepest and most fascinating issues which all those engaged in studying, teaching or developing the subject should be concerned with.

This work is a study of the meta-theory or methodology of legal theory. As the theoretical wing of an intensely practical discipline, legal philosophy sometimes appears to be undergoing

---

[1] Woody Allen, "My Apology" in W. Allen, *Side Effects* (London, New English Library Ltd, 1981), 40–1.

a perpetual identity crisis, its self-conception and aspirations unclear, even in jurisprudential writings of the highest calibre.[2] As a result, what I regard as vital and deeply fascinating questions are frequently left unanswered. What are we trying to achieve in constructing theories of law and by what criteria may we account such theories as successful? On what basis do and/or should we adjudicate between rival jurisprudential claims, and/or the theories which make those claims? Are the aims of a theory of law descriptive, or critical, or justificatory with regard to its explanandum? Are any or all of these approaches mutually antagonistic, or could, for example, a descriptive approach to legal theory be compatible with a justificatory account of the nature of law? Is there a correct method via which law should be understood in order to achieve one or more of the aims mentioned above?

All legal theorists take an implicit stance on meta-theoretical or methodological questions such as these. Few, however, address such matters directly, and to the extent to which this does occur, the authors concerned often confine themselves to some relatively brief remarks in the course of pursuing some other agenda.[3] This

[2] There are, of course, some exceptions to this state of affairs. For examples of legal theorists adopting a more self-reflective stance as regards their task, see e.g. H.L.A. Hart, "Definition and Theory in Jurisprudence" (1954), 70 *Law Quarterly Review* 37, reprinted in H.L.A. Hart, *Essays in Jurisprudence and Philosophy* (Oxford, Clarendon Press, 1983); J. Raz, "The Problem about the Nature of Law", first published in (1983) 3 *Contemporary Philosophy: A New Survey*, and (1983) 21 *University of Western Ontario Law Review* 203, and reprinted in J. Raz, *Ethics in the Public Domain* (Oxford, Clarendon Press, 1994).

[3] See e.g. W. Waluchow, *Inclusive Legal Positivism* (Oxford, Clarendon Press, 1994), ch. 2, which deals with the topic of methodology in legal theory in the service of better elucidating certain aspects of Dworkin's position. I do not wish to denigrate Waluchow's contribution to this topic which I regard as an interesting one, nor more generally to criticise those who include discussions on methodology within works dealing primarily with other matters. My point is merely that there are few sustained treatments of methodology in legal theory, and that, in my view, jurisprudence could benefit from the debate which would be engendered by the existence of some more extended works on this topic. Recent years have witnessed some positive developments in this area, with several writers in the field taking a more sustained interest in questions concerning

failure to deal with matters meta-theoretical head-on and in a systematic way has resulted in some serious misunderstandings as regards the aspirations and point of certain theories of law, both amongst the general readership of such theories, and even as between certain legal theorists themselves. This book, then, takes the topic of methodology in legal theory as its chief concern, and seeks to address that topic by raising to the surface and subjecting to critical discussion some presuppositions about the nature of jurisprudence which often remain buried in various contemporary approaches to understanding law.

Proceeding in such a manner, however, still leaves a vast amount of ground which could potentially be covered by the present work, such that some kind of organising principle remains necessary in order to determine where the focus of the inquiry should lie. In the course of what follows, then, I approach some of the presuppositions about jurisprudential methodology which legal theorists implicitly endorse via an examination of one particular meta-theoretical theme, namely the role of evaluation in legal theory. The central question motivating this examination is as follows: to what extent, and in what sense, must a legal theorist make value judgements about the phenomena which he seeks to characterise in order to construct a successful theory of law? In the remainder of this section, I attempt to flesh out further the nature of and reasons behind asking this question.

Although various other discussions feature in the book, a substantial part of it is concerned with a comparative analysis of the role of evaluation in the respective legal theories of John Finnis,

the criteria of success of theories of law. See e.g. S.R. Perry, "Interpretation and Methodology in Legal Theory", in A. Marmor (ed.), *Law and Interpretation* (Oxford, Clarendon Press, 1995); S.R. Perry, "Hart's Methodological Positivism" (1998) 4 *Legal Theory*, 427); J.L. Coleman, "Incorporationism, Conventionality, and the Practical Difference Thesis", in (1998) 4 *Legal Theory* 381 and J.L. Coleman, *The Practice of Principle: In Defence of a Pragmatist Approach to Legal Theory* (Oxford, Oxford University Press, forthcoming, March 2001), part three; G.J. Postema, "Jurisprudence as Practical Philosophy" in (1998) 4 *Legal Theory* 329.

Ronald Dworkin, and Joseph Raz. The starting point for this analysis is the idea that legal theory has traditionally been understood as encompassing a distinction between those theorists who assert or deny respectively that it is possible to have an adequate account of law, "as it is" which is distinct from an account of how it ought to be. Where it is necessary to do so, I shall refer to this distinction as "the is/ought distinction".[4] A little background may prove useful here, in introducing the particular jurisprudential chestnut which many of the discussions in this book seek to address.[5]

The is/ought distinction probably owes much of its contemporary fame to the writings of Jeremy Bentham, and to Bentham's separation of expositorial from censorial jurisprudence in particular. Bentham famously objected to the confusion between law "as it is" and law as it morally ought to be which he discerned in Blackstone's *Commentaries on the Law of England.*[6] In Bentham's view, this confusion resulted in Blackstone presenting an account of law as being morally meritorious in the course of offering an exposition of law as it actually was, and hence being unwilling to offer criticism of existing law.[7]

---

[4] The distinction is sometimes rendered as being between descriptive theories of law on the one hand, and normative theories on the other. I shall say more about this way of characterising the distinction, and about the problems which it can engender, at the beginning of Chapter 2.

[5] The interested reader may also wish to consider Hart's discussion of the history of the is/ought distinction in H.L.A. Hart, "Positivism and the Separation of Law and Morals" (1958) 71 *Harvard Law Review* 593, and reprinted as essay II in H.L.A. Hart, *Essays in Jurisprudence and Philosophy* (n. 2 *supra*).

[6] See J. Bentham, Preface to the 1st edn. of *A Fragment on Government, or a Comment on the Commentaries*, in *The Works of Jeremy Bentham*, Vol I, published under the superintendence of John Bowring (Edinburgh, W. Tait, 1838–43), especially at 227–30. For present purposes, I would also refer readers to H.L.A. Hart's excellent commentaries on and discussions of Bentham's work in H.L.A. Hart, *Essays on Bentham* (Oxford, Clarendon Press, 1982). On expositorial and censorial jurisprudence, see in particular 1–2, 41 and 137 of this latter work. The essay by Hart mentioned in the preceding note is also relevant in this respect.

[7] See H.L.A. Hart, "Positivism and the Separation of Law and Morals" (n. 5 *supra*); H.L.A. Hart, "The Demystification of the Law", in Hart, *Essays on Bentham* (n. 6 *supra*), essay I.

Bentham, on the other hand, firmly believed that one could not assume from the simple fact that something was law that it inevitably also possessed moral merit. For Bentham, one could have good law and one could have bad law, but all such phenomena shared some features in common which rendered them law. These common features lay not in law's substantive merit (or demerit), but rather in its structure or form: put very crudely, that law is the posited will of a Sovereign law-giver.[8] For Bentham, then, law as it is and law as it ought to be were to be considered separately: expounding law as it is was the task of expositorial jurisprudence; criticising the law in the name of its future improvement and reform was the job of the censorial jurist concerned with law as it ought to be.[9]

Interestingly, Bentham's views on this matter were driven by a censorial or moral end: he believed that the critique and subsequent reform of the law which formed the core of the censorial jurist's task could only be achieved once he had an accurate description or exposition of law "as it is" i.e. demystified and stripped to its essentials.[10] In this way, for Bentham, the moral aims of censorial jurisprudence provided the motivation for engaging in expositorial jurisprudence, and rendered this latter an essential precursor to the vital task of law reform. This aspect of Bentham's position was also adopted by his fellow nineteenth century jurist, John Austin, although, as commentators have

[8] See J. Bentham, *Of Laws in General* (H.L.A. Hart (ed.), London, Athlone Press, 1970), chs I and II. NB. the crudeness refers to my necessarily brief characterisation of nineteenth century "command" theories of law (and indeed of commentaries thereon).

[9] See also J. Bentham, *Introduction to the Principles of Morals and Legislation* (J.H. Burns and H.L.A. Hart (ed.), London, Athlone Press, 1970), ch. XVII, ss 21–9. These brief introductory remarks gloss over many complex issues regarding Bentham's distinction between expositorial and censorial jurisprudence, and concerning his methodological position more generally. For further discussion of these issues, see G.J. Postema, "The Expositor, the Censor, and the Common Law" (1979) 9 *Canadian Journal of Philosophy* 643; G.J. Postema, *Bentham and the Common Law Tradition* (Oxford, Clarendon Press, 1986), 304–36.

[10] Once again, see Hart, "The Demystification of the Law", in Hart, *Essays on Bentham* (n. 6 *supra*), essay I.

noted, Austin exhibited significantly less interest in the task of the censorial jurist than did Bentham himself.[11] Austin's position on the question underlying the is/ought distinction—can you have an adequate account of law, "as it is" which is distinct from an account of how it ought to be—is captured in his oft-quoted remark, "the existence of law is one thing; its merit or demerit is another".[12]

Bentham and Austin thus both subscribed to a principle which has an important bearing on how we ought to go about constructing theories of law. The principle in question claims that the study of law as it is can and should be kept separate from the study of law as it ought to be. Moreover, especially in Bentham's case, this principle was supplemented by the view that the latter enterprise may be assisted by first undertaking the former one in the proper manner.

Twentieth century jurisprudence began by holding good to this central methodological insight of its nineteenth century forerunners. For Hans Kelsen, however, the view that the study of law as it is should be kept separate from the study of law as it ought to be was combined with a belief that the latter activity is not within the remit of the discipline of jurisprudence at all, as: "the task of the science of law is not to approve or disapprove of its subject, but to know and describe it".[13] This particular aspect of Kelsen's views is, of course, in contrast with Bentham, who regarded the jurist as being concerned both with knowing and describing the law, and with approving or disapproving of

---

[11] For an introductory discussion, see e.g. Cotterrell, *The Politics of Jurisprudence: a Critical Introduction to Legal Philosophy* (London, Butterworths, 1989), 52–7. This point is somewhat controversial, however, and readers wishing to examine it further might also consider E. Ruben, "John Austin's Political Pamphlets 1824–1859" in E. Attwooll (ed.) *Perspectives in Jurisprudence* (Glasgow, University of Glasgow Press, 1977), and cf. W.L. Morison, *John Austin* (London, Edward Arnold, 1982), ch. 4.

[12] John Austin, *The Province of Jurisprudence Determined* (London, Weidenfeld and Nicholson, 1955 (1832)), 184.

[13] H. Kelsen, *The Pure Theory of Law*, 2nd edn. trans. M. Knight (Berkeley, Ca., University of California Press, 1967), 68. For Kelsen's views on methodology more generally, see *The Pure Theory of Law*, 2nd edn., chs I–III.

it, albeit whilst wearing different "hats" (expositorial or censorial respectively) and whilst engaging in different kinds of jurisprudential enterprise.

H.L.A. Hart's work is also cast in the Benthamite methodological mould. That his is a "general and descriptive"[14] theory of law which is, "morally neutral and has no justificatory aims"[15] is, according to the author himself, implicit throughout his jurisprudential writings. More explicitly, the delineation of this methodological stance forms an important part of Hart's comments on the differences between his own position and that of Ronald Dworkin in the first section of the posthumously published "Postscript" to *The Concept of Law*.[16]

Since Hart, however, there have been twentieth century legal theorists who wish to call into question the distinction between descriptive and justificatory jurisprudence. For example, some theorists offer accounts of law which rest on the methodological premise that in order adequately to characterise law "as it is", a legal theorist must necessarily take a stance on the moral merit or demerit of the law. On this kind of view, the task of characterising law "as it is" is necessarily and inextricably bound up with one's understanding of how law morally ought to be, such that the two enterprises cannot be separated in the way in which Bentham, Kelsen and Hart advocated. The accounts of law espoused by John Finnis and Ronald Dworkin both exemplify this approach, albeit in very different forms.[17] What both accounts share, however, is that they reject the thesis that the social institution of law can simply be described, "as it is", and embrace the notion that legal theorists cannot characterise law adequately unless they offer an account of the point, purpose or function of law, in terms of the values, often rendered as moral

---

[14] H.L.A. Hart, *The Concept of Law*, 2nd edn., with a postscript edited by P.A. Bulloch and J. Raz (Oxford, Clarendon Press, 1994), 239.

[15] Hart, *The Concept of Law*, 2nd edn. (n. 14 *supra*), 240.

[16] Hart, *The Concept of Law*, 2nd edn. (n. 14 *supra*), 239–44.

[17] See R. Dworkin, *Law's Empire* (London, Fontana Press, 1986); J. Finnis, *Natural Law and Natural Rights* (Oxford, Clarendon Press, 1980), and the discussions of these works in Chapters 2 to 6.

7

values, which law serves. Finnis and Dworkin thus deny that law can—as Bentham, Kelsen, Hart and also Joseph Raz seem to contend—be adequately characterised in terms of the institutional structures and procedures via which it operates (e.g. in terms of the union of primary and secondary rules) and insist instead that it is only by coming to certain conclusions regarding the wider moral value, purpose or point of law (for example, that it should operate so as properly to constrain governmental coercion (Dworkin), or that it should provide the framework conditions which will allow us to realise certain values or basic goods in our lives for ourselves (Finnis)) that we can adequately understand what it is.

In summary: according to the usual way of understanding the is/ought distinction in legal theory, many theorists in the legal positivist camp, including Bentham, Austin, Hart, Kelsen, and Raz, stand together in asserting that it *is* possible to have an adequate account of law, "as it is" which is distinct from an account of how it ought to be. Finnis and Dworkin, on the other hand, are held to disagree and to deny that descriptive and normative/justificatory jurisprudence can be separated in this way. One of my main concerns in this work, however, is that the matter is not so simple as these initial formulations of it would have us believe, owing to the fact that the is/ought distinction in fact encompasses several different issues which are often confused and/or inadequately understood, and which I seek here to separate out and subject to critical analysis.

As I already indicated, in the present work, I contend that these issues can best be approached via the theme of the role of evaluation in legal theory, and more specifically, via the question: to what extent, and in what sense, must a legal theorist make value judgements about the phenomena which he seeks to characterise in order to construct a successful theory of law? The (at least *prima facie*) link with the is/ought distinction should be quite obvious, for it might be assumed that if a legal theorist is engaging only in descriptive jurisprudence concerned with law as it is, then he need not make any value judgements at all concerning that which he seeks to characterise in his theory. Conversely, it might seem to follow that those theorists who, like Finnis and Dworkin, adopt an approach to jurisprudence which denies that we can simply describe law as it is, will necessarily be involved in making judgements about the moral value, point or function of the law in order to characterise it adequately. On such a view, then, theorists giving respectively affirmative or negative answers to the question: can we have an adequate account of law "as it is" which is distinct from an account of how it ought to be?, also give the same respectively affirmative or negative answers to the question: can legal theory be value-free?

I regard such conclusions as at best misleading, and at worst downright false. Moreover, I believe that such conclusions are in part engendered by the overly simplistic way in which the is/ought distinction has traditionally been understood. This being so, in order to explore further the role of evaluation in legal theory and the connection between this topic and the is/ought distinction, I propose to separate out certain of the individual methodological questions which the distinction encompasses, and to discuss each of these in turn.

For present purposes, then, there are three main senses in which the is/ought distinction can be understood, namely as demarcating the positions of those theorists who assert or deny respectively that:

(1) in order to understand law adequately, a legal theorist must morally evaluate the law (I will refer to this as the **moral evaluation thesis**);

(2) in order to understand law adequately, a legal theorist must hold the law to be a morally justified phenomenon (the **moral justification thesis**); and,

(3) value judgements concerning the beneficial moral consequences of espousing a certain theory of law may legitimately feature in the criteria of success of legal theories (the **beneficial moral consequences thesis**).

One of my main tasks in the book is to consider each of the above theses in turn, and to locate the views of various contemporary legal theorists in terms of them. In the discussions which follow, I devote most of my time and attention to the first of the three theses, i.e. the moral evaluation thesis. The reason for this is that it is through an examination of this thesis that I can best bring out the nature of the methodological approach to legal theory which I regard as the correct one. That said, however, and as will become apparent in the course of what follows, considering the other two theses mentioned above also forms an important, albeit very much a secondary, part of my present analysis of the role of evaluation in legal theory.

As has already been mentioned, this analysis proceeds in the main via a comparison of Finnis' and Dworkin's respective stances on the criteria of success to which legal theories should aspire, with the methodological position adopted by Joseph Raz. Raz rejects all three theses listed above, but nonetheless maintains that legal theory cannot be value-free. I believe that Raz's stance exemplifies the correct sort of methodological position for a legal theorist to adopt, and that this position is not well understood at present. The existence of such misunderstandings is evidenced by Finnis and Dworkin's claims that the Razian position has no ground which it can coherently occupy, and hence must inevitably collapse into some variant of their own respective positions.[18] Attempting to explain the nature and significance of the kind of methodological position which I attribute to Raz—and which I term **indirectly evaluative legal theory**—can thus be viewed as the main focus of the discussions in this book. It should be noted that my aim is to characterise this methodological position in general, not merely in the form in which it is instantiated in Raz's particular account of the nature of law. However, because Raz's methodological position can be used in order to illuminate the indirectly evaluative approach to legal theory, the present work proceeds in large part by attempting to bring out the nature of this approach via examining Raz's stance, and considering whether it can be defended from criticisms which have been or could be levelled at it. It is important to mention, however, that in this work I do not necessarily

[18] These claims are discussed in Chapters 2 to 6.

endorse all of the elements in Raz's methodological position, or all of the arguments which he uses in order to support his particular view of the nature of law. Rather, I am using those aspects of his position which are discussed here in order to illustrate what I regard as the correct sort of approach to understanding law. My interest, then, lies with the kind of arguments which Raz makes, rather than with their substantive detail. The extent to which I am in agreement with those arguments should be clear from the context in which they are discussed. Moreover, it should also be noted that I do not know whether Raz would agree with my interpretation of his views as presented here.

Although undertaking a comparative analysis of the methodological positions of Finnis, Dworkin and Raz represents a primary task of the book, various other discussions do feature in it, and the overall intention is to present the reader with some views on the criteria of success of legal theories, which, although he may disagree with them, will hopefully provide him with some provocative food for thought in approaching and considering methodological issues for himself. In this way, the book seeks to develop several interesting conversational gambits as regards the topics with which it deals, in the hope of tempting others to join in the debate. In keeping with this aim, and also driven in part by some of the considerations raised in section B of this chapter, the book does not attempt to adjudicate conclusively between alternative jurisprudential methodologies, nor itself to develop a fully fledged meta-theory of legal theory. Rather, it will be successful to the extent that it assists in deepening our understanding of the matters with which it deals, and insofar as the views expressed within it help to engender rigorous and focused debate as regards the nature of theorising about law.

B. Some Remarks on the Methodology of Methodology

This work is self-proclaimedly "meta" in terms of its subject matter: it is primarily concerned not with the nature of law but with the nature of theorising about law. This being the case, some readers may have doubts about the possibilities for and value of the project which I have outlined even before they come to examine the substance of the views expressed herein. Such doubts may come in various guises. For example, some may object to works purporting to deal with jurisprudential methodology not because of any substantive claims which they make, but because of a suspicion that their very existence indicates a malaise elsewhere within the discipline. According to the line of thinking which I have in mind, there is an inversely proportional relationship between developments in the substance of a discipline, and interest in it at a meta level, such that when one waxes, the other must inevitably be on the wane; interest in jurisprudential methodology flourishing when there is a lack of progress in substantive accounts of the nature of law.[19] I very much hope that a concern with matters meta-theoretical does not betray a lack of interest in or inspiration as regards first order jurisprudential theories, both so far as the present author is concerned, and/or as regards the state of the discipline as a whole. Indeed, for reasons which should become apparent in the course of this work, some of which are indicated below, I regard under-standing the nature of law and understanding the nature of legal theory as complementary and mutually enhancing activities, rather than as occupying opposite positions on some jurisprudential wheel of fortune.

In any case, even if there were to be some truth in this particular law of inverse proportion, whilst it may augur ill for the state of our theories of law, it does not strike directly at the aspirations of a project like the present one. More important in this regard, then, is the objection that such a project is fundamentally flawed for the reason that one cannot come to any important conclusions about correct jurisprudential methodology without delving deep into and attempting to come to the

---

[19] Andrei Marmor briefly considers whether this phenomenon may partially explain why, until recently, there has been a relative lack of interest in methodology in jurisprudence, i.e. because of the substantive leaps forward which Hart and those following in his wake brought to the discipline. See A. Marmor, *Interpretation and Legal Theory* (Oxford, Clarendon Press, 1992), 2.

correct conclusions about the nature of law itself. The force of this line of attack lies in the thought that there can be little or no value in a work which deals purely or even perhaps primarily with jurisprudential methodology, as the truth and explanatory adequacy of the views expressed within it can only be gauged by undertaking an examination and evaluation of the substance of the accounts of law which are supported by various of the methodological approaches which the work discusses.

In responding to this objection, the first point to mention is that, for the most part, the present work leaves unexplored the issue of the extent to which jurisprudential methodologies can be evaluated on their own, i.e. without considering them in conjunction with the substance of the theories which they support. In order to illustrate the relevance of this point, we can briefly consider two possible models of the relation of methodologies to the theories which rest upon them. According to the first model, the correctness of a given methodological approach is independent of and prior to the correctness of the substantive account of law which is generated according to it. That is to say, on this model, it will be possible to adjudicate between alternative jurisprudential methodologies on purely methodological grounds, and the success of a theory of law will be dependent on its at least adopting what has, on methodological grounds, first been determined to be the correct jurisprudential methodology.

The second model is more holistic in nature, holding that methodologies and the theories which they generate must be evaluated together, and that each can derive support from the success of the other. On this second model, then, a given methodology can gain support from the appeal of the theory which it generates, for example, from how well that theory accords with our pre-theoretical understanding of the phenomena under investigation.[20]

[20] Note that there may be other possible models of the relations between theories of law and their methodological foundations, and that, as regards the models which I do mention, those relations may be much more complex than can be discussed in this brief sketch. Nonetheless, I hope that the distinction, as drawn

If the first model is the correct one, then the objection considered above can be fully rebutted, and the various arguments in favour of or against certain jurisprudential methodologies which feature in the course of this work could potentially be conclusive in nature, and would not necessarily require further support from arguments regarding which theory of law yields the most convincing account of that social institution in terms of, for example, our pre-theoretical understanding of it. As I mentioned above, this work leaves this issue largely unexplored, but, in fact, I tend to lean much more toward the second model of the relation between methodologies and the theories which are generated according to them. This being the case, and as I cannot within the confines of the present project also conduct an adequate investigation into which substantive jurisprudential theory yields the most convincing account of the law, I accept that my discussion of various jurisprudential methodologies is unlikely to be conclusive in nature. In other words, there is a limitation upon the present project stemming from the fact that it is most likely not possible to adjudicate conclusively between the various methodological approaches which I examine without also delving into many other questions regarding the correctness of the theories of law which those methodologies support.

However, while this much may be conceded to the objector, it should not lead us to conclude that there is little or no value in undertaking a project such as the present one. The reason for this is that, even on the second model of the relation between theories of law and the methodologies which support them, I would contend that it is possible to identify some issues and concerns which are distinctively methodological in nature. In light of this point, I would further argue that even if, as I suspect, the second model is correct, then although the arguments contained in this book are most likely not conclusive, they will speak to that part of the debate between legal theories which is concerned with methodology. The arguments marshalled to provide sup-

above, is useful in terms of indicating how much work I take the discussions in the rest of the book to be capable of doing.

port for or criticism of various jurisprudential methodologies will not be the final word on the matter, then, but they can illuminate the nature of those methodologies, and go some way toward providing reasons for or against adopting a given approach. Moreover, in light of what I regard as the lack of adequate discussion of these questions, I believe that, even if not conclusive in nature, the analyses which I undertake here are of value in deepening our understanding of the nature of legal theory in general, and of the methodological presuppositions underlying certain theories of law in particular.

C. A Closer Look at the Task of Analytical Jurisprudence

As the remarks in the previous two sections should make clear, I do not attempt to elaborate or defend a fully fledged metatheory of legal theory in this book. That said, however, in this introductory chapter, I do wish to offer a schematic account of what I take the criteria of success of a legal theory, or, at any rate, of a legal theory of a certain type, to be. This account draws upon recent work on this topic by Joseph Raz,[21] and, it must be emphasised, is a presentation rather than a vindication of the task of a certain type of legal theory. The reasons for proceeding in this way are two-fold. First of all, I wish to indicate some aspects of my stance on correct jurisprudential methodology at the outset in the hope that this will allow the reader better to understand and engage with the discussions which follow. Secondly, and perhaps more importantly, I believe that it is necessary to proceed in this way in order to provide a framework which adequately sets the parameters for the various substantive discussions with which the book is concerned.

The following account, then, should be viewed both as an initial statement of my position on the aspirations of legal theory, and as a kind of map of the relevant meta-theoretical terrain

[21] In the main, I draw upon J. Raz, "Can There Be a Theory of Law" (manuscript, Oxford, 2000), and J. Raz, "On The Nature of Law" (1996), 82 *Archive für Rechts und Sozialphilosophie* 1.

15

which I use to locate and highlight the significance of the various discussions which form the substance of this work. I am of course aware that many aspects of this account are controversial and that some readers will disagree strongly with it. However, bearing in mind the remarks made above concerning the purpose of setting the scene via such an account, I would ask those who have doubts about the view of the task of legal theory which I am about to present not to condemn this project for that reason at the outset, but rather to use the account provided in order to open up the territory of what follows, and so better enable them to engage, critically or otherwise, with the substantive discussions and arguments of this book which form its explanatory core.

In considering what the task of jurisprudence might be, a preliminary issue to be considered is the sheer number of areas of intellectual inquiry and questions therein which, at one time or another, and in one way or another, have been included within the ambit of this discipline. To list but a few examples, issues relating to criminology, the sociology of the judiciary, legal anthropology, methods of alternative dispute resolution, behaviourist accounts of the relation between law and other types of social norms, and even the role of artificial intelligence in legal reasoning, can be viewed as falling within the scope of theorising about law. In some of these cases, shades of interdisciplinarity evidently add to the potential variety in both subject matter and approach. Moreover, theoretical issues abound in any inquiry which is conducted at a sufficient level of abstraction, with the result that almost any subject in the corpus of black-letter law of a given jurisdiction can be addressed in a jurisprudential way. All of this is to say nothing of the vast array of critical legal scholarship which seeks to denounce more traditional ways of conceiving of law, or of theorising about it.

Given this almost overwhelming heterogeneity, it seems that it will not be possible to come to any useful conclusions about the task of jurisprudence unless the ambit of that which is being addressed can be curtailed quite drastically. In the present work, I concentrate upon an approach to theorising about law which is often referred to as analytical jurisprudence. However, I present a view of the ground which this tradition occupies, and of that which is included within its ambit, which may be at odds with some commonly held intuitions on this matter. In the main, this is due to my belief that this approach is most fruitfully characterised in terms of the criteria of success to which a theory of law of a certain type aspires, rather than in terms of the subject matter with which it deals, or the kind of view of that subject matter which it adopts.[22]

What, then, are the criteria which demarcate a good or successful analytical jurisprudential theory?[23] In short, analytical jurisprudence is concerned with explaining the nature of law by attempting to isolate and explain those features which make law into what it is. A successful theory of law of this type is a theory which consists of propositions about the law which (1) are necessarily true, and (2) adequately explain the nature of law.[24] Points (1) and (2) are intimately linked: a theory's ability to explain adequately the nature of law is dependent upon its at least consisting of necessarily true propositions. As will be discussed shortly, however, this is only a necessary, not sufficient condition of the explanatory adequacy of such an approach.

On this characterisation of it, analytical jurisprudence is concerned with accurately and adequately explaining the nature of law. This notion of "the nature of law" may require a little further elaboration. In this work, I am using "the nature of law" to refer to those essential properties which a given set of phenomena must exhibit in order to be law. The task of analytical jurisprudence, then, is to search for and explain those properties

[22] This is explained further below.

[23] Although there are many valuable alternative approaches to understanding law, in this work I am not concerned with the criteria of success of theories which do not fit the analytical jurisprudential model.

[24] This formulation, although paraphrased slightly, is taken from Raz, "Can There Be a Theory of Law?" (n. 21 *supra*), section 1. It would be far beyond the scope of this work to enter into a discussion of the kind of necessity which might be in play here. Fortunately, this is not required in order to give a presentation of the analytical jurisprudential approach which is adequate for present purposes.

17

of law which make it into what it is. Such properties are evidently ones which law, at any time, and in any place, must exhibit. This being the case, another way of characterising the task of analytical jurisprudence is to say that it is concerned with the nature of law in the abstract, as opposed to the way in which it is instantiated in particular legal systems.[25]

It might be asked why a successful theory of law of this type need consist of propositions about the law which are necessarily, as opposed to merely contingently, true. The answer to this is that only necessarily true propositions about law will be capable of explaining the nature of law. If law has a given feature, but this is discovered to be a contingent matter, due, for example, to the social and/or economic conditions which just happen to hold sway in a particular time and place, and hence is not necessary to its existence as law, then the feature in question is not one which is part of law's essential nature, and cannot assist us in the important task of getting to the heart of this social institution in the sense of understanding that which makes it into what it is.

Perhaps, however, a would-be challenger could then claim that in restricting successful analytical jurisprudential theorising to that which can deliver such necessary truths, we are begging the very question which we seek to investigate, and assuming that law *has* essential properties. This, our challenger might add, is a wildly implausible assumption. The correct response to this move is to point out that no such question has yet been begged, because the approach as delineated so far does not state nor assume that the law in fact has essential properties. Instead, it is merely stipulated that, *if* there are such properties, then a successful legal theory of the type under consideration would have to find them. Turning this point around, it would follow that one reason why it might be impossible to have a successful theory of law of this type is simply that law does not possess any essential properties. In terms of the discussion so far, this possibility remains open. This being so, the challenger can re-cast his

[25] Once again, I draw upon Raz, "Can There Be a Theory of Law?" (n. 21 *supra*), section 1.

original point in the form of a claim that the task of analytical jurisprudence is a futile one as the law does not in fact possess any essential properties. This, however, will have to be demonstrated by showing the inability of theories of law of the type under consideration to find and explain any essential properties in the case of law, and not merely by claiming that such theories are wrong, or question-begging, in their attempt to do so.

For some, however, all of this will still smack of a kind of essentialism which they may believe to be philosophically misplaced in general, and *a fortiori* in the case of the philosophy of a man-made social institution such as law. Once again, I cannot fully vindicate my view of the task of analytical jurisprudence here. I will, however, just offer a final few words in its defence. The approach just set out does not claim that legal systems are necessary features of all human societies, nor that all human societies have thought of law in the same way.[26] The point is merely this: given that we regard there as being something special about certain forms of social organisation which we account as legal, and given that we recognise that, throughout history, some forms of social organisation have amounted to legal systems and some have not, the only way in which we can begin to investigate what this particular form of social organisation is like, and how it differs from other types of social organisation, is by attempting to isolate and explain those features which are constitutive of it, and which make it into what it is. Such features can be nothing more nor less than law's essential properties, and it will be necessarily true that law exhibits such properties.

[26] For a discussion of the compatibility of the thesis that different societies, at different times, have had different concepts of what law is/have thought of law in different ways, with the search for law's essential properties, see Raz, "Can There Be a Theory of Law?" (n. 21 *supra*), section 4, and Raz, "On The Nature of Law" (n. 21 *supra*), *passim*. As the remarks above indicate, there are many other interesting questions to be tackled in this area. These, however, are beyond the scope of the present discussion which attempts merely to present as much of an account of the nature of analytical jurisprudence as is necessary in order to provide a point of focus for the discussions of jurisprudential methodology with which this work is concerned.

This characterisation of analytical jurisprudence leaves open many questions, including the question of how numerous the law's essential properties might be. I do not propose to say too much on this topic, because leaving the matter open in this way is entirely appropriate: we cannot know what law's essential properties are or how numerous they might be without engaging in particular lines of first order analytical jurisprudential inquiry, a project which is ongoing over time. Given that law is a complex and multi-faceted social phenomenon, however,[27] we would seem to have no reason to believe that such properties will be few in number and indeed it is at least possible that there may be an indefinite number of such properties. This possibility is one of the reasons motivating my previous suggestion that analytical jurisprudence should be thought of as being delimited in terms of criteria of success rather than subject matter or attitude towards subject matter. The criteria of success model allows for the plausible possibility that law could possess an indefinite number of essential properties, different sub-sets of which could be identified and explained by investigation in any one of the numerous subject matter areas mentioned at the outset of the present discussion. On this view, then, analytical jurisprudential inquiry may concern itself with various of the subject matters previously mentioned, and may adopt various attitudes in respect of them.

The criteria of success model also accords well with the view of analytical jurisprudence which I endorse because I believe that there are many instances in which it would be overly restrictive, question-begging, and unhelpful to exclude certain inquiries from the province of analytical jurisprudence on grounds relating to the subject matter which they address, or the kind of view of that subject matter which they adopt. To take an example which illustrates that which is intended by this latter category: I would regard as overly restrictive and question-begging any move to define all possible critical approaches to understanding law as being in a separate camp from analytical

[27] The wide variety of ways of characterising law previously listed testify to this.

jurisprudence.[28] The reason for this is that I do not believe that we should exclude at the outset the possibility that one of law's essential properties could be something which would render the law an essentially unjust phenomenon which we should thus be critical of. For example, perhaps it is possible that helping to sustain a false consciousness which contributes to the continued exploitation of the labouring classes by those who own the means of production is one of law's universal and essential properties. A theory which made this claim and which argued as a result that law is an essentially unjust phenomenon would be attempting to explain the nature of law by elucidating its essential properties. If the claim were true (and I do not contend that it is) and adequately explained a certain aspect of the nature of law, then the theory would meet the criteria of success of an analytical jurisprudential theory. Contrariwise, it is possible that the essential properties of law are such as to render it a morally valuable or morally justified social institution. In my view, and as is discussed further in Chapter 2, John Finnis is one proponent of analytical jurisprudence who reaches just this conclusion with respect to the central case or focal meaning of law. According to the view presented here, then, what marks a theory as falling within the ambit of analytical jurisprudence is not *which* essential properties it claims the law possesses, but *that* it regards law as having such properties, and that it conceives of the task of a legal theory as being to identify and explain what they are.

It is the type of enterprise outlined above which I take, for example, Thomas Aquinas, Jeremy Bentham, John Austin, H.L.A. Hart and Hans Kelsen to have been conducting, and which John Finnis and Joseph Raz are engaged upon today. Noticeably absent from this roll call of the Jurisprudence Hall of Fame is, of course, Ronald Dworkin. Certain aspects of Dworkin's position cause difficulties in terms of placing his work within the tradition of analytical jurisprudence as just characterised. Arguably, Dworkin

[28] On the characterisation offered here, much critical legal scholarship will be excluded from the ambit of analytical jurisprudence. My point is that this is due to features of such scholarship other than the bare fact that its aims are primarily critical.

cannot be regarded as a proponent of this approach because his account of law commits him to the view that legal theory cannot be universal in the sense presupposed by analytical jurisprudence. Owing to the fact that it consists of an interpretation of them, Dworkin's theory of law is contingent upon the particular legal practices of a specific society. Moreover, it seems that the kinds of societies whose legal practices can be interpreted in the manner which Dworkin has in mind are "our" kind of society, i.e. liberal democracies such as the United Kingdom or USA which are committed to individual rights and to the virtues of justice, fairness and procedural due process which play such a significant role in the Dworkinian vision of how law is to be interpreted. On this view, Dworkin's theory of law is thus intended as an account of law in those types of society only.[29]

Moreover, whether or not Dworkin intends his theory to have universal application, it is certainly the case that his views run counter to the analytical jurisprudential approach in the sense that he treats attempts to account for the nature of law in the abstract, and attempts to answer the question of what the law requires in particular legal situations as part of one continuous enterprise. That is to say, for Dworkin, the question "what is the nature of the social institution of law?" and the question, "is A entitled to receive damages from B?" are the same in kind, differing merely as regards the level of abstraction at which they are asked and ought to be answered.[30] According to proponents of analytical jurisprudence, however, this latter kind of question depends upon the way in which the law is instantiated in particular legal systems, and is a separate matter from the

[29] See, in particular, Dworkin, *Law's Empire* (n. 17 *supra*), 216: "I am defending an interpretation of our own political culture, not an abstract and timeless political morality". This point is, however, a matter of controversy in Dworkin scholarship which cannot be settled conclusively here. For further views on this issue, see e.g. P. Soper, "Dworkin's Domain" (1987) 100 *Harvard Law Review* 1166; J. Raz, "Can There Be a Theory of Law"'(n. 21 *supra*), section 4 and cf. J. Raz, "Two Views of the Nature of the Theory of Law: a Partial Comparison" (1998) 4 *Legal Theory* 249, at 281–2.

[30] See Dworkin, *Law's Empire* (n. 17 *supra*), 90, and the discussion of Dworkin's position in Chapters 5 and 6.

22

characterisation of the nature of law in the abstract.[31] Dworkin does not recognise this alleged qualitative distinction between questions concerning the nature of law in the abstract, and those concerning its realisation in particular legal institutions, and this leaves us, perhaps, in terminological difficulties, for it seems to indicate that Dworkin's work should be excluded from analytical jurisprudence as characterised in the foregoing discussion. This, however, is problematic, because he is evidently one of the central contributors to twentieth century jurisprudential thought, and, moreover, his work, as much as any of those mentioned above, seeks to characterise law accurately and adequately. (Although, as various of the discussions in the book indicate, he has a unique view of how we should go about achieving that aim.)

These points take us right to the heart of some of the issues which are dealt with in Chapters 5 and 6 of the book, and, on the whole, are best postponed until the discussions of Dworkin's views undertaken in those chapters. Insofar as the purely terminological point goes, however, the view which I take is that, as Dworkin's approach represents such a major new departure for legal theory, it does not seem helpful to agonise over whether to classify it as lying wholly or partly within or outwith the analytical jurisprudential tradition. This being the case, I concentrate my energies in Chapters 5 and 6 upon analysing and criticising the substance of certain of Dworkin's views on jurisprudential methodology, in order to bring into focus the points at which they conflict with the view of legal theory with which I wish to ally myself—the classificatory niceties I leave for others.

In concluding this presentation of the task of analytical jurisprudence, it is important to note that a successful theory of this type must do more than feature *any* chosen sub-set of necessarily true propositions explaining those properties which something must possess in order to be law. This is due to the

[31] Andrei Marmor holds the recognition of such a distinction to be the defining feature of analytical jurisprudence, and hence sharply contrasts Dworkin's position with this approach, see Marmor, *Interpretation and Legal Theory* (n. 19 *supra*), 35.

fact that some such sub-sets will not fulfil the second criterion of a successful theory of this sort, namely that it must adequately explain what law is. This further criterion of explanatory adequacy is vital in adjudging as successful the type of legal theory under consideration. What I have in mind is the simple yet vitally important point that it is necessary for any such theory to deal with the data which it purports to characterise in a way which is appropriate to, and adequate in respect of, the nature of that data.

This point should not appear overly mysterious, for it is in fact very familiar to us in the context of the development of legal theory in the twentieth century. One of the great advances in the discipline was H.L.A. Hart's insistence on the importance of an understanding of rules in characterising legal phenomena, and of understanding those rules from the point of view of those who are subject to, use and apply them.[32] This shift of emphasis illuminated a whole range of data which was inadequately dealt with by earlier versions of legal positivism, which, even in their more sophisticated manifestations, offered "external" accounts of legal phenomena.[33] Such accounts were inadequate because they failed to understand law from the internal point of view, i.e. as it is understood by those who are subject to it and who use it to guide their behaviour.

That Hart's achievement was such a significant one rests on the vitally important methodological precept referred to above: that it is necessary for a legal theory to approach the data which it seeks to characterise in a way which is appropriate to the nature of that data, on pain of otherwise offering a distorted account of it. In the case of rules, which are centrally important in understanding the nature of law, this requires providing an account which adequately incorporates the internal point of

[32] See Hart, *The Concept of Law*, 2nd edn. (n. 14 *supra*), *passim*, but perhaps especially 51–61, and 82–91.

[33] In *The Concept of Law* (n. 14 *supra*), Hart's illustrative fall-guy in this regard is John Austin, but the arguably more sophisticated version of the "command" theory of law propounded by Jeremy Bentham can also be criticised for the same reason.

view. This point explains why the requirement that a good or successful theory of law must consist of necessarily true propositions is not the last word as regards its explanatory adequacy; why truth is merely a necessary, not sufficient condition in this respect.[34] Jurisprudential theories must not merely tell us truths, but must tell us truths which illuminate that which is most important about and characteristic of the phenomena under investigation. Moreover, in so doing, those theories must be sufficiently sensitive to the way in which those living under the law regard it.[35]

D. A Guide to the Book's Structure

Chapter 2 of the book opens with a preliminary discussion of some of the pitfalls of understanding the jurisprudential methodological scene in terms of the is/ought or descriptive/normative distinction. The main task of this chapter, however, is to examine the first of the three issues which I introduced in section A of the present chapter, namely whether a legal theorist must morally evaluate the law in order to understand it adequately (to recap: for shorthand purposes, I term this the moral evaluation thesis). The discussion of this issue proceeds via a comparative analysis of John Finnis' and Joseph Raz's views on this topic, and seeks to explain the sense in which Finnis endorses, while Raz rejects, the moral evaluation thesis. As the chapter unfolds, it reveals a puzzle or problem which will have to be solved if the Razian approach is to survive the sorts of criticisms which Finnis levels at it.

Chapter 3 attempts to provide the necessary solution to this puzzle. The discussion in this chapter introduces some

---

[34] To the extent that they consist of necessarily true propositions (and, once again, I am not claiming that they do), Marxist theories of law may be good examples of theories which are true, but explanatorily inadequate, owing to the fact that they do not deal with how legal rules appear to those who are subject to them and who use them as standards of conduct.

[35] This point is dealt with in greater depth in Chapter 2.

important distinctions between approaches to legal theory which are followed through and developed in the remainder of the book. In particular, I am concerned to flesh out the kind of approach to legal theory which Raz adopts, and to explain how this position acknowledges and indeed embraces the thesis that legal theory cannot be value-free, whilst rejecting the contention that the evaluation involved must necessarily be moral evaluation. Unravelling the features of this methodological position—which, once again, I term indirectly evaluative legal theory—can be viewed as the main thread of argument which runs throughout the book.

Chapter 4 then goes on to deal, albeit briefly, with Finnis' stance on the second of the three issues introduced in section A of the present chapter, namely whether a legal theorist must hold law to be a morally justified phenomenon in order to understand it adequately (the moral justification thesis). The chapter also explores the relation between this issue and the moral evaluation thesis.

Chapter 5 functions as a kind of bridge in the book, between Finnis' challenge to indirectly evaluative legal theory discussed in the three chapters preceding it, and Dworkin's challenge which is examined in Chapter 6. This chapter introduces and explores the third issue mentioned in section A above, namely whether value judgements concerning the beneficial moral consequences of espousing a certain view of law may legitimately feature in the criteria of success of legal theories. The reasons for dealing with this issue within this bridging chapter, and before returning to an examination of the moral evaluation and moral justification theses in relation to Dworkin's position, are two-fold. First of all, this issue (the beneficial moral consequences thesis) is sometimes confused with the first of the three main issues which the book addresses, namely whether a legal theorist need morally evaluate the law in order to understand it adequately. This being the case, I believe that the contrast between the two issues can best be brought out by first discussing the moral evaluation thesis, and then introducing and explaining the beneficial moral consequences thesis immediately thereafter. Secondly, one of the main arguments which I discuss in approaching the beneficial moral consequences thesis, namely that proffered by Frederick Schauer in his article, "Positivism as Pariah",[36] provides a useful lead-in to Ronald Dworkin's position, and, in particular, to understanding how Dworkin's methodological stance relates to the beneficial moral consequences thesis. Chapter 5 thus opens with a discussion of the beneficial moral consequences thesis in general terms, and then moves to a consideration of the relevance of this issue in beginning to understand Dworkin's methodological stance, thus forming a kind of bridge to Dworkin's views.

Chapter 6 of the book deals further with Dworkin's views on correct jurisprudential methodology. The chapter begins with an examination of Dworkin's position in terms of the moral evaluation and moral justification theses respectively. I then go on to consider the relation of Dworkin's stance on the moral evaluation and moral justification theses to his view regarding the point or function of law. The chapter also addresses the issue of whether, in general, legal theorists need to take a stance on law's overall point or function in order to construct an accurate and adequate legal theory. The main aims of the chapter are to provide a critical analysis of Dworkin's views on this issue, and to indicate the sense in which the indirectly evaluative approach to legal theory does not require us to understand law as performing a particular moral function in order to provide an adequate account of it.

In the final chapter of the book, I attempt to sum up some of the conclusions reached in the course of the discussion so far, and to elaborate still further upon the nature of indirectly evaluative legal theory, and upon the reasons for adopting such a methodological approach.

As well as discussions of the methodological positions of Finnis, Dworkin and Raz, I do also attempt from time to time, often in the notes to this work, to locate my views in relation to those of other commentators in the field who have lately

[36] F. Schauer, "Positivism as Pariah", in R.P. George (ed.), *The Autonomy of Law: Essays on Legal Positivism* (Oxford, Clarendon Press, 1996).

expressed an interest in matters methodological. Despite this, however, the constraints and goals of the present project dictate that I cannot pretend to offer a detailed analysis of any particular commentator's views or an in-depth examination of exactly how or why my own account departs from them. So far as the present work is concerned, this comparative task is left mainly to the interested reader, and can only be achieved by a careful reading of the account of correct jurisprudential methodology which I offer in this book, and then by comparing it with the views of those theorists discussed or mentioned in this work, and/or others. Such an approach is in keeping with my hopes for the work as a whole, which are that it will both provide the beginnings of answers to some existing questions, and also raise new ones, encouraging others to carry on the conversation.

2
Introducing the Moral Evaluation Thesis

A. Introduction

In Chapter 1, I introduced the central question driving the discussions in this book, namely, to what extent, and in what sense, must a legal theorist make value judgements about the law in order to construct a successful analytical jurisprudential theory? I also stated that I intend to approach this question by examining three distinct issues which are sometimes obscured by focusing on the more traditional methodological controversy of whether we can have an adequate account of law "as it is" which is distinct from an account of how it ought to be. To recap: the issues in question are:

(1) in order to understand law adequately, is it necessary to morally evaluate the law? (or, to put it another way: must a successful legal theorist subscribe to the moral evaluation thesis?);

(2) in order to understand law adequately, is it necessary to hold the law to be a morally justified phenomenon? (or, must a successful legal theorist subscribe to the moral justification thesis?); and

(3) can value judgements concerning the beneficial moral consequences of espousing a certain view of law legitimately feature in the criteria of success of legal theories? (or, can a legal theorist legitimately subscribe to the beneficial moral consequences thesis?)

This chapter addresses the first of these three questions. Much light can be shed on this methodological issue by comparing the views of Joseph Raz and John Finnis with regard to it, and so this will form the basis of my approach here. The chapter also sets up a puzzle or problem which must be solved if the Razian methodological approach is to successfully rebut the challenges which Finnis levels at it. My attempted solution to that puzzle is postponed until Chapter 3. Before embarking upon my examination of these matters, however, I want to say a preliminary word or two on why I regard the question underlying the is/ought distinction[1]—can you have an adequate account of law "as it is" which is distinct from an account of how it ought to be?—as unhelpful, and why, therefore, it is better to address the topic of the role of evaluation in legal theory by investigating the three distinct issues demarcated above.

B. Evaluation and Legal Theory: Some Popular Myths

One main reason why I regard the question underlying the is/ought distinction—can you have an adequate account of law "as it is" which is distinct from an account of how it ought to be?—as problematic, is because it assumes that opinion on this issue is divided into just two methodological camps. This both fails to do justice to the complexity of the meta-theoretical issues which the question is intended to address, and often leads to serious misrepresentations of the views of some legal theorists. The two camps are sometimes dubbed "descriptive" and "normative" jurisprudence respectively, with those who would answer the above question in the affirmative allegedly falling into the former camp (e.g. Bentham, Austin, Hart, Kelsen, and Raz), and those answering in the negative (e.g. Finnis and Dworkin) being placed in the latter.[2] As many of the discussions in the book attempt to illustrate, the "two camps" model as it is usually understood is overly simplistic and fails to capture some

---

[1] See p. 4 *supra* for my use of this term.

[2] Some form of this descriptive/normative classificatory schema (sometimes rendered as a distinction between descriptive-explanatory legal theory and

important distinctions between theories and theorists as regards their views on correct jurisprudential methodology.

Another difficulty with carving things up in this way is that those doing so sometimes appear to assume that the difference between these alleged two camps is the difference between value-free legal theories on the one hand, and value-laden legal theories on the other. According to this line of thinking, those who are customarily regarded as "descriptive" legal theorists, e.g. Bentham, Hart and Raz, are thought by some to claim that it is possible to have an account of law which is entirely value-free: "the most satisfactory jurisprudential theories turn out not to be purely descriptive and value-free, as Hart claimed".[3]

Taken at face value, such a claim would be to the effect that a legal theorist need not involve himself in making any value-judgements whatsoever in the course of constructing an adequate account of the nature of law. This is false in both a rather banal, and a more important sense. That is to say, there are two ways in which evaluative judgements play a part in legal theories such as Hart's and Raz's. However, as is argued throughout the book, it is important to realise that neither of these two ways in which, for example, Razian legal theory involves evaluative

---

normative-justificatory legal theory) is at work in many contemporary discussions concerning jurisprudential methodology: see e.g. S.R. Perry, "Interpretation and Methodology in Legal Theory", in A. Marmor (ed.), *Law and Interpretation* (Oxford, Clarendon Press, 1995); S.R. Perry, "Hart's Methodological Positivism" in (1998) 4 *Legal Theory* 427; G.J. Postema, "Jurisprudence as Practical Philosophy" in (1998) 4 *Legal Theory* 329. H.L.A. Hart also made reference to some version of this dichotomy in seeking to explain the distinction between his own methodological position, and that of Ronald Dworkin, in section I of his posthumously published "Postscript" to H.L.A. Hart, *The Concept of Law*, 2nd edn., with a postscript edited by P.A. Bulloch and J. Raz (Oxford, Clarendon Press, 1994). In recent work, Jules Coleman also criticises the use of the normative/descriptive dichotomy in characterising methodological debates in legal theory, see J.L. Coleman, *The Practice of Principle: In Defence of a Pragmatist Approach to Legal Theory* (Oxford, Oxford University Press, forthcoming, March 2001), Introduction and ch. 12.

[3] Perry, "Interpretation and Methodology in Legal Theory", in Marmor (ed.), *Law and Interpretation* (n. 2 *supra*), 100.

judgements, renders this type of theory "normative" in the sense in which this term is usually intended, i.e. to denote the kind of position, adopted by Finnis and Dworkin, which claims that we cannot have an adequate account of law without engaging in *moral* evaluations of it, and, in particular, moral evaluations of law's overall point or function. Despite being evaluative in both a banal, and a more than banal sense, then, the methodological position which I attempt to elucidate throughout this work, and which I term indirectly evaluative legal theory, does not require legal theorists to morally evaluate (nor morally justify) the law, in the manner of Finnis' and Dworkin's theories, in order to characterise it accurately and adequately. It should be obvious, then, why this position does not sit well within the descriptive/normative classificatory schema, or the value-free/morally evaluative dichotomy which is often presented as underlying it. This being so, the present work comes armed with a plea that we should give up classifying legal theories in terms of this unhelpful descriptive/normative terminology.

The force of these statements, and the arguments which underlie them will, I hope, become clearer as the discussions in this chapter, and in the book as a whole, proceed. To begin to illuminate them, let us start with the more banal sense in which legal theory cannot be value-free. If we reflect upon the question of what it is that a theory—any theory—is trying to do, then certain conclusions seem inevitable. For instance, it seems a commonplace to point out that theories seek to make and communicate arguments coherently and effectively; that they aim to put their message across in a way which will allow those encountering the theory to understand as fully as possible what the theory is trying to convey. This being so, there are several virtues which a theory ought to have and to strive toward possessing, such as simplicity, clarity, elegance, comprehensiveness and coherence. I wish to term such virtues "purely meta-theoretical values". The reasons for using this term will be discussed further shortly, but for now, it is sufficient to register that such virtues are ones which it is valuable for a theory concerning any subject matter whatsoever to exhibit, and that this is due simply to the nature of theories; in particular, to the fact that they seek to communicate arguments effectively.

I am claiming, then, that virtues such as simplicity, comprehensiveness and clarity are ones which it is valuable for any theory, including a legal theory, to possess.[4] This state of affairs means that legal theorists who wish to communicate arguments effectively, as much as theorists of any other sort, must necessarily be in the business of making evaluative judgements in the course of constructing their theories so as to ensure that they exhibit these virtues to the highest possible degree. That legal theories such as H.L.A. Hart's which are usually characterised as "descriptive" are necessarily evaluative in *this* sense is in fact recognised by many commentators on this topic. So when some such commentators report that an allegedly descriptive theory claims to be value-free, what they in fact seem to mean is that although construction of the theory must obviously involve purely meta-theoretical value judgements such as those mentioned above, nonetheless the theory can still be characterised as "descriptive" if it does not require any evaluation going beyond this "banal" level in order to be successful. "Descriptive" legal theories are thus not characterised as entirely value-free, but rather as relatively value-free: they obviously involve purely meta-theoretical evaluation, but they do not take those constructing them into the territory of, for example, morally evaluating the law in order to provide an accurate and adequate account of it.

An example of this sort of characterisation of "descriptive" legal theory emerges in the course of Stephen Perry's discussion of whether H.L.A. Hart's methodological stance is best viewed as an example of what Perry terms a "descriptive-explanatory" approach:

"The descriptive-explanatory method assesses theories by means of criteria that are properly called evaluative, such as predictive power

---

[4] On this point, see also Wil Waluchow, *Inclusive Legal Positivism* (Oxford, Clarendon Press, 1994), 19–29.

and simplicity, but the values in question are applicable to all scientific theories, and they are not normative in character".[5]

The fact that it is taken for granted that such "innocent"[6] or purely meta-theoretical evaluation inevitably features in theories falling on the "descriptive" side of the descriptive/normative divide, would already seem to give us reason to eschew this dichotomy in favour of other ways of characterising the distinctions between types of legal theory, given the "value-free" connotations which the term "descriptive" sometimes engenders. Moreover, in considering the place of purely meta-theoretical values in legal theory, we are already beginning to discuss one of several distinct issues regarding the role of evaluation in legal theory which are better dealt with as exactly that, i.e. as individual issues, rather than being masked behind the overly simplistic descriptive/normative dichotomy. However, as will be discussed below, the real ills of the descriptive/normative classificatory schema are not apparent until we examine how those making use of it tend to characterise those theories which step over what they regard as the "descriptive" side of the divide and are hence classified as "normative".

Perry states in the passage quoted above that purely meta-theoretical values such as simplicity are applicable to all scientific theories. In fact, I regard such values as being applicable to theories concerning any subject matter whatsoever, as they do not bear upon the truth of the particular substantive claims which a given theory makes, but are rather concerned with optimal ways of getting the message of the theory across, and are hence considerations which apply irrespective of what the content of that message might be.[7] This begins to explain why these values can

---

[5] Perry, "Hart's Methodological Positivism" (n. 2 *supra*), 438. Later in this article, Perry comes to reject the idea that Hart should be characterised as a descriptive-explanatory legal theorist.

[6] The adjective is borrowed from Gerald Postema, who uses it in discussing the role of evaluation in H.L.A. Hart's legal theory, in Postema, "Jurisprudence as Practical Philosophy" (n. 2 *supra*), at 333.

[7] This may also be what Perry intends, as it is not clear to me exactly what he

be termed "purely meta-theoretical", i.e. because they relate only to the nature of theories in general, rather than to the nature of the particular data or explananda with which a given theory or type of theory deals. Furthermore, this also begins to explain why I have termed such evaluation "banal". If we are to learn something interesting about the role of evaluation in *legal* theory, then we must seek to understand whether, and in what sense, the particular data with which legal theory deals has a special bearing upon the kinds of evaluative judgements which a successful legal theorist must make. Discussions of the role of evaluative considerations in theories concerning any subject matter whatsoever, while of interest up to a point, do not yet tell us anything particularly special or important about the enterprise of understanding law.

These points are implicitly recognised by Perry in the course of his characterisation of H.L.A. Hart's approach to legal theory as going beyond such "innocent" purely meta-theoretical evaluation: "Hart is making evaluative claims not about theories, but about the very social practices he is studying".[8] The point which Perry seeks to make here is an extremely important one, and indeed it is a large part of my task in this work to illustrate the sense in which the approach to legal theory which I support, indirectly evaluative legal theory, does require evaluative judgements which concern the particular social practice which is studied by theories of law. Moreover, I also believe that Perry is quite correct in arguing that Hart, too, is making evaluative judgements about the social practices he is studying.[9] However, it is

means by the term "scientific" in this context. See Perry, "Hart's Methodological Positivism" (n. 2 *supra*), 436–8.

[8] Perry, "Hart's Methodological Positivism" (n. 2 *supra*), 438. See also 456–7 of the same article. Postema also mentions this point in Postema, "Jurisprudence as Practical Philosophy" (n. 2 *supra*), 334.

[9] In the article from which the above quotation is taken, Perry rightly draws our attention to the fact that Hart himself may not have realised this. So far as my own view of the matter goes: although in this book, I use Raz's as opposed to Hart's work in order to provide illustrations of the approach to jurisprudential methodology which I support, in fact, I regard Hart as being committed, whether he realised it or not, to many of the same methodological tenets as

the direction which Perry's views on correct jurisprudential methodology take following this observation which indicates what I described previously as the real ills of the descriptive/normative classificatory schema.

Perry's view is that all legal theories, in order to be adequate to their task, must go beyond "innocent" purely meta-theoretical evaluation, and make evaluative judgements about the particular data with which legal theory deals, i.e. the social practice of law. However, he then goes on to claim that once legal theories do overstep the limits of purely meta-theoretical evaluation, then in order to be in with a chance of success, they must inevitably end up being "normative" in nature, which, according to Perry's own understanding of that term, means that they are evaluative in the sense that they involve: "moral and political argument intended to show which theory makes the best moral sense of the social practice we call law".[10]

Moreover, for Perry, theories which engage properly in such moral and political argument are allied, methodologically speaking, with Ronald Dworkin's particular approach to legal theory, such that they proceed by:

> "showing how the practice, construed in terms of a certain point or function that might plausibly be attributed to it, could under specified conditions give rise to moral obligations for participants which they would not otherwise have. The idea is to make moral sense of the practice by showing people why and under what circumstances they might have reason to comply with it".[11]

Much of Perry's work on jurisprudential methodology is dedicated to examining Hart's position and the internal tensions which he believes it contains, and the discussions which he offers us in this regard are subtle and fine-grained in nature,

---

Raz. Unfortunately, the work necessary to establish this cannot be undertaken here. For an illuminating discussion of the role of evaluation in Hart's account of law, see L. Green, "The Concept of Law Revisited" (1996) 94 *Michigan Law Review* 1687, section IV.

[10] Perry, "Hart's Methodological Positivism" (n. 2 *supra*), 466.

[11] Perry, "Hart's Methodological Positivism" (n. 2 *supra*), 463.

such that I cannot do justice to them here. Perry does not exactly claim that Hart must inevitably collapse into Dworkin,[12] methodologically speaking, or that there are no other tenable methodological positions in legal theory apart from the purely meta-theoretical evaluation of what he terms a "descriptive-explanatory approach"[13] on the one hand, and Dworkinian methodology on the other. Rather, his contention is that once, as any explanatorily adequate legal theory must,[14] you move beyond the purely meta-theoretical evaluation featuring in a descriptive-explanatory approach, then in order to have a legal theory which is adequate to its task, and, in particular, adequate to that part of its task which consists in explaining law's normativity, it is necessary to adopt a "normative" approach which involves morally evaluating the law in order to make the best moral sense of it, in terms of the overall point or function which that social institution is taken to serve.[15]

My contention in this work is that this latter claim is false. Legal theories do and must involve evaluative judgements which are more than purely meta-theoretical in nature, and which concern the particular kinds of data/social practices which those theories attempt to explain. However, it is not the case that, by so doing, those theories are involved in *morally* evaluating the law, and nor do or should they seek to show law in its best moral light according to some overall point or function which they ascribe to it. There is, we might say, some further ground regarding the role of evaluation in legal theory which Perry seems not to have discovered, and which I suspect the influence of the descriptive/normative dichotomy has helped to keep concealed. It is this ground which is occupied by the indirectly evaluative approach to legal theory which this book seeks to examine. Having

[12] Although he does claim that, "the seeds of Dworkin's strong version of interpretivism were sown by Hart himself" in Perry, "Interpretation and Methodology in Legal Theory" (n. 2 *supra*), 101.

[13] Perry, "Hart's Methodological Positivism" (n. 2 *supra*), 429.

[14] This point is examined further in the following section.

[15] See Perry, "Hart's Methodological Positivism" (n. 2 *supra*), and Perry, "Interpretation and Methodology in Legal Theory" (n. 2 *supra*), *passim*.

preliminarily staked out the boundaries of the territory in question, then, we now turn to its fuller elucidation and analysis.

C. Evaluation and Legal Theory: All or Nothing at All?

As I stated in the introduction, this chapter is concerned with the first and, for present purposes, perhaps most important[16] of the three methodological issues which lie at the heart of this inquiry, namely whether it is necessary to morally evaluate the law in order to construct an explanatorily adequate legal theory.[17] In this section, I compare John Finnis' and Joseph Raz's views on this issue, in order to begin to shed some light upon it. Finnis and Raz agree that evaluation on the part of the legal theorist is essential for any explanatorily adequate theory of law, but, as we shall see, they have very different ideas about what is involved in such evaluation.

In the opening chapter of *Natural Law and Natural Rights*, Finnis decisively rejects the idea that legal theory can be "value-

[16] See p. 10 *supra*.

[17] To avoid the possibility of confusion between the question of the identification of the content of the law (i.e. the question which legal positivism answers in the form of the social thesis, see e.g. Hart, *The Concept of* Law, 2nd edn. (n. 2 *supra*), 100–10 and 250; J. Raz, *The Authority of Law* (Oxford, Clarendon Press, 1979), ch. 3), and the question of how to go about identifying and characterising the social institution of law (i.e. the question which this work claims should be answered by adopting the indirectly evaluative methodological approach to legal theory), let me make clear the following. In this work, I am treating these two questions as separate, and, unless indicated otherwise by the context of the discussion (as is the case, for example, at some points in Chapters 5 and 6, where I discuss certain arguments in favour of legal positivism's social thesis), I am discussing factors relating to the characterisation of the social institution of law, i.e. the latter sort of question just mentioned. Some theorists of course, most notably Ronald Dworkin, do not accept that the questions can be separated in this way. Dworkin's view on this matter is extremely relevant to present concerns and will be considered in Chapters 5 and 6.

free", pointing out that theory construction inevitably involves evaluative work on the part of the theorist, because:

> "there is no escaping the theoretical requirement that a judgement of *significance* and *importance* must be made if theory is to be more than a vast rubbish heap of miscellaneous facts described in a multitude of incommensurable terminologies".[18]

As it stands, however, this point amounts to no more than the thought that any theorist must assess or evaluate which are the most important features of the data to be explained, on pain of presenting a collection of unconnected miscellaneous facts instead of a coherent argument in the form of a theory. As such, this "theoretical requirement", as Finnis calls it, merely involves the theorist in purely meta-theoretical value-judgements which are applicable to theories concerning any subject matter whatsoever and which do not yet tell us anything particularly interesting about the task of *legal* theory. Indeed, as presented by Finnis in this passage, the requirement seems no more than an elucidation of what it is for something to *be* a theory at all, rather than the presentation of a "rubbish heap" of facts.

This, however, does not get to the heart of Finnis' views in the opening chapter of *Natural Law and Natural Rights*. In that chapter, Finnis makes a further claim about the way in which evaluative considerations of importance and significance are woven into the particular type of enterprise which *legal* theorists are engaged upon, owing to the nature of the data with which legal theory is concerned. This further claim is apparent in Finnis' contention that a legal theorist must not merely pick out and explain the important or significant facets of his data, but that in so doing, he must:

> "assess importance or significance in similarities and differences within his subject-matter by asking what would be considered important or significant in that field by those whose concerns, decisions and activities create or constitute the subject-matter".[19]

[18] John Finnis, *Natural Law and Natural Rights* (Oxford, Clarendon Press, 1980) (hereinafter *NLNR*), 17 (emphasis in original).
[19] Finnis, *NLNR* (n. 18 *supra*), 12.

This point is vital in the present context, and is elaborated further by Joseph Raz in the following passage:

"Legal theory contributes . . . to an improved understanding of society. But it would be wrong to conclude, as D. Lyons has done, that one judges the success of an analysis of the concept of law by its theoretical sociological fruitfulness. To do so is to miss the point that, unlike concepts like 'mass' or 'electron', 'the law' is a concept used by people to understand themselves. We are not free to pick on any fruitful concepts. It is a major task of legal theory to advance our understanding of society by helping us to understand how people understand themselves.

To do so it does engage in evaluative judgement, for such judgement is inescapable in trying to sort out what is central and significant in the common understanding of the concept of law."[20]

As these passages indicate, Raz and Finnis agree that legal theory involves evaluation on the part of the theorist. Their remarks also reveal that, in their view, the evaluation in question amounts to something more than the purely meta-theoretical evaluation discussed in the previous section. This "something more" is evident from their insistence that there are certain methodological consequences for *legal* theory which arise from the fact that the data which that discipline seeks to explain is of a particular nature. What both Raz and Finnis seek to bring to our attention is that the data or subject matter which legal theory addresses is itself already shot through with evaluations of what is important and significant about it, because that data partly consists in beliefs and attitudes about the law and actions in light of the law on the part of those subject to it. This point turns out to have great significance in terms of how legal theorists should go about their task.

As Raz mentions in the passage quoted above, there are some important differences between types of concepts which can feature in theoretical explanations. Raz frames one such distinction as being between concepts which are already used by people to

[20] J. Raz, "Authority, Law and Morality", in J. Raz, *Ethics in the Public Domain* (Oxford, Clarendon Press, 1994), 210–37, at 237 (internal reference omitted).

understand themselves, and those which are not. The significance of the distinction is that, in the former case, because the concept to be explained is one which is already used by people in characterising and comprehending their own behaviour and beliefs, this results in certain methodological consequences for someone seeking to offer a theoretical account of that concept. This point is important for legal theory because law is one such concept which people use to understand themselves. This being so, a theory of law's ability to account accurately for and explain adequately beliefs about and attitudes towards the law on the part of those who are subject to it, and who understand their social world partly in terms of it, is a centrally important criterion in determining whether it is a good account of this social institution.

In illustrating this point, Raz contrasts law with two concepts used extensively in physics, but this does not mean that he intends his distinction to track whatever differences there may be between concepts in the natural as opposed to the social sciences, because (amongst other reasons) we can also find examples from the social sciences of concepts which are not used by people in order to understand themselves. For instance, in that branch of criminology known as "strain theory", Robert K. Merton employs a five-fold classification of individuals' modes of adaptation to strain caused by restricted access to socially approved goals and means. The concepts involved in Merton's classificatory schema can be used to characterise types of human behaviour and attitudes, but those concepts are not already used by those to whom they are applied in order to understand their own behaviour and attitudes.[21] Take, for instance, Merton's concept of "ritualism". According to Merton, "ritualism" occurs where an individual who is frustrated as regards his access to certain goals rejects those goals themselves and instead focuses

[21] Merton's five modes of adaptation are: conformity, innovation, ritualism, retreatism and rebellion. See Frank P. Williams III and Marilyn D. McShane, *Criminological Theory*, 2nd edn. (Englewood Cliffs, NJ, Prentice-Hall, Inc., 1994), ch. 6; Robert K. Merton, *Social Theory and Social Structure*, revised and enlarged edn. (New York, NY, Free Press, 1968).

on the alleged means by which they are supposed to be achievable:

> "In this mode the means can become the aspirations of such an individual, as when one may attempt to treat a job (means) as a form of security instead of using the job as a means of achieving success. In this example, keeping the job has become a goal by itself, resolving the frustration of unsuccessfully chasing the original goal".[22]

Those who display the behaviour and attitudes which are picked out by Merton's concept of ritualism are unlikely to be aware of their status in the eyes of passing criminological strain theorists, or to have views on what is important or significant about ritualism as a mode of adaptation because, apart from those well-versed in the ways of criminology, persons generally do not have recourse to the concept of ritualism in understanding themselves. This being the case, when a criminological strain theorist such as Merton introduces and explains the concept of ritualism, he need be guided only by concerns such as how fruitful the introduction and elucidation of this concept will prove in terms of facilitating his research programme: it is not the case that there are widespread pre-existing understandings of ritualism amongst those whose behaviour he is attempting to characterise which he must adequately account for and explain in elucidating this concept.

Things are very different in the case of the concept of law. The overwhelming majority of persons living in a society governed by law are aware of this social institution, and have views concerning what it is like, and what is important about it. They know, for example, that one of the important things about law is that it can employ coercive force against you; that if you disobey it, you can ultimately be physically confined or have some of your possessions forcibly removed. Similarly, people are aware that the law is not an optional system of conduct-guidance, such as yoga, or freemasonry. It is not something which one signs up for, but rather is compulsorily applicable to

[22] Williams III and McShane, *Criminological Theory*, 2nd edn. (n. 21 *supra*), 92.

all falling within its jurisdiction, with or without their approval. In light of this awareness of what law is like, people often also develop views on whether and in what circumstances they ought to obey it. That the concept of law is thus already part of the conceptual currency which we use to understand our social world means that the legal theorist is not in the same position as a criminology theorist seeking to elucidate the concept of ritualism. The legal theorist does not introduce a concept anew in order to further his account of the behaviour of persons not familiar with that concept. Rather s/he seeks to elucidate a concept which people already know about and make use of in characterising the society in which they live, and their own behaviour and attitudes within it. This being the case, any explanatorily adequate legal theory must, in evaluating which of law's features are the most important and significant to explain, be sufficiently sensitive to, or take adequate account of, what is regarded as important or significant, good or bad about the law, by those whose beliefs, attitudes, behaviour, etc. are under consideration. The legal theorist is thus not merely engaging in evaluative judgements regarding that which is important and significant about his data, as any theorist must, but is making evaluative judgements regarding what is important and significant about law which take account of, and attempt to explain, the way in which it is viewed by those living under it.

In making these remarks, it is important to note that I am not trying to over-intellectualise the kind of views about the law held by those subject to it, nor to underplay the task of legal theorists in attempting to explain those views and their significance for understanding the nature of law. Analytical jurisprudence does much more than merely report on views about the law held by those subject to it, attempting as it does to systematise, clarify, sieve for importance and relevance and incorporate them into a cogent and persuasive account of the nature of law. Moreover, the views of those subject to the law are of course not held in anything like the form in which they appear in jurisprudential writings. The point is merely that analytical jurisprudence has a responsibility to the views about law held by those subject to it in a sense which results in particular methodological consequences for this discipline.

To return to our main discussion: Finnis and Raz thus both agree that in order to construct an explanatorily adequate legal theory, it is necessary to make evaluations regarding that which is important or significant about the social practice to be explained. Moreover, this is not merely purely meta-theoretical evaluation which applies in respect of theories in general, but rather is evaluation which is concerned with the particular kind of data with which legal theory deals, i.e. the social practice of law, and with the fact that the nature of that practice, in particular, that it includes people's understandings of themselves in terms of law, has a significant bearing upon what will count as success in legal theory. In order to construct a successful analytical jurisprudential theory, then, a theorist must make sound evaluative judgements regarding that which is important to explain about law which take adequate account of how law is understood by those living under it, and must offer illuminating explanations of those important features.

Finnis' next move in this debate is to point out that part of what makes up the self-understandings and evaluations of members of a society subject to law are understandings of the law's links with morality; these, too, are simply part of the data to be explained by a theory of law. For example, the law invariably claims that it has legitimate moral authority, and on this basis demands the obedience of those to whom it is addressed. That is to say, it is in the nature of law that it presents itself using moral terminology such as authority, duty, obligation and right, and claims to state how people really ought to behave. Moreover, where a legal system is in force, many people, perhaps especially the officials of that system, believe the law's claims to be justified, and this point of view, that of someone who believes that the law dictates what people really ought to do, would seem to be one which it is very important for a legal theory to explain.[23]

---

[23] Again, see Finnis, *NLNR* (n. 18 *supra*), ch. I, *passim*, but especially 13–14.

Raz's position is in keeping with Finnis' as regards the need for a theory of law to explain people's understandings of the law as having authority over them:

> "it is in the nature of law that it claims authority over its subjects, and it is treated as law by and large only by people who accept that claim. To understand it we have to understand what it claims to be and what it is taken to be by those who accept its claims".[24]

It is at this point, however, that Raz and Finnis' positions diverge. Although both agree that a legal theorist must make evaluations of that which is important about his subject matter, and although they further concur that those evaluations must be sufficiently sensitive to the way in which those subject to the law understand and evaluate it, including, where they have them, to their understandings and evaluations of it as a moral phenomenon, Finnis wishes to make two distinct further claims which Raz challenges. Those claims are that: (1) in order to evaluate which are law's important features, and to explain those features, the legal theorist must morally evaluate the law, and (2) that such an evaluation will lead to the conclusion that the law is a morally justified phenomenon which lives up to its claims that it is morally legitimate and ought to be obeyed.

Regarding the first point:[25] Finnis' view appears to be that once the process of evaluating what is important about law has begun, there is, so to speak, no place to stop and a legal theorist must morally evaluate the law in order to understand it adequately.[26] He contends that in order to identify and give an account of certain important features of the law, the theorist will not merely have to pick out as important and explain certain

---

[24] J. Raz, "On the Nature of Law" (1996) 82 *Archive für Rechts und Sozialphilosophie* 1, at 13. See also Raz, *The Authority of Law* (n. 17 *supra*), ch. 2; Raz, "Authority, Law and Morality", in Raz, *Ethics in the Public Domain* (n. 20 *supra*), 210–37.

[25] The second is discussed in Chapter 4.

[26] The reader should note that some of my presentation of Finnis' views in this chapter is drawn from his elaboration of it in seminars given within the Law Faculty of the University of Oxford during the period October 1994–March 1997, rather than purely from the text of *NLNR* (n. 18 *supra*).

self-understandings and beliefs about the law held by those subject to it, but will himself have to assess and take a stance on the
correctness of those self-understandings and beliefs.[27] As law's
important features include its claim to moral legitimacy and the
acceptance of this claim by many of those subject to it, Finnis
contends that it is only through assessing the correctness of
those claims and attitudes, and thus attempting to understand
whether and under what conditions the law's claims, and
acceptance of them, really are justified, that a theorist can give
an adequate account of the nature of law. The reason for this,
according to Finnis, is that such an assessment is necessary for
us to be able to understand the focal meaning or central case of
law.[28] For Finnis, this is characterised in terms of law's function,
which is to guide properly the conduct of those subject to it
according to certain principles of practical reasonableness and
so resolve the co-ordination problems of a community for the
common good of that community:[29]

> "the evaluations of the theorist himself are an indispensable and deci-
> sive component in the selection or formation of any concepts for use
> in the description of such aspects of human affairs as law or legal
> order . . . the theorist cannot identify the central case of that practi-
> cal viewpoint which he uses to identify the central case of his sub-
> ject-matter unless he decides what the requirements of practical
> reasonableness really are".[30]

In Finnis' view, then, the legal theorist cannot merely pick out
as important and explain certain features of the law, such as its
claim that it is morally authoritative, and the acceptance of
that claim by some of those subject to it, as the Razian position

[27] See Finnis, *NLNR* (n. 18 *supra*), 13–18.

[28] Finnis, *NLNR* (n. 18 *supra*), 9–11.

[29] Finnis, *NLNR* (n. 18 *supra*), *passim*, but perhaps especially chs I to VI, IX,
X and XII. The constraints of the present work dictate that it is not possible to
offer a fuller account of the various elements in Finnis' position, or of the inter-
relations between them. For a comprehensive elucidation of the Finnisian project, the interested reader should consult Finnis' *Natural Law and Natural Rights*
(n. 18 *supra*) for himself.

[30] Finnis, *NLNR* (n. 18 *supra*), 16–17.

maintains. Rather, <u>for Finnis, the theorist must decide whether</u> ✳
<u>the law's claims are true, and their acceptance justified, and</u>
must characterise law from the "central case" viewpoint of one
subject to it who makes the correct judgements concerning the
requirements of practical reasonableness, and the role of the law
with regard to them:

> "Among those who, from a practical viewpoint, treat law as an aspect
> of practical reasonableness, there will be some whose views about
> what practical reasonableness actually requires in this domain are, in
> detail, more reasonable than others. Thus the central case viewpoint
> itself is the viewpoint of those who not only appeal to practical rea-
> sonableness, but also are practically reasonable".[31]

Moreover, according to Finnis, the theorist who goes through
this process of correctly identifying the central case of law will
come to the conclusion that the law's claims that it is morally
legitimate and ought to be obeyed, *are* true, such that:

> "If there is a point of view in which legal obligation is treated as at
> least presumptively a moral obligation . . . then such a viewpoint will
> constitute the central case of the legal viewpoint . . . such a viewpoint
> is the viewpoint which should be used as the standard of reference
> by the theorist describing the features of the legal order".[32]

For Finnis, then, a legal theorist must inevitably wade deep
into the waters of moral evaluation, for a legal theory will be successful to the extent that it correctly identifies what the requirements of human practical reasonableness truly are, and to the
extent that it understands law as having the function of helping
us to realise those requirements, such as to create a moral obligation to obey it.

Raz's position, on the other hand, is that <u>although evaluation</u>
<u>of the law must necessarily enter into any adequate jurispruden-</u>
<u>tial theory, the evaluation concerned is not moral evaluation</u>. For
example, in discussing the way in which evaluative considerations are woven into his defence of the sources thesis, he tells us
that:

[31] Finnis, *NLNR* (n. 18 *supra*), 15.
[32] Finnis, *NLNR* (n. 18 *supra*), 14–15.

> "It turns on evaluative conceptions about what is significant and important about central social institutions, i.e. legal institutions. But in claiming that these features are important one is not commending them as good . . . while this is an evaluative judgement, it is not a judgement of the moral merit of anything".[33]

It thus seems that Raz wants to have one kind of evaluation going on in his theory, namely the type of evaluation which allows the legal theorist to identify which are the most important and significant amongst the attitudes, beliefs and self-understandings of those subject to the law, but not another, namely a moral evaluation of the substance or content of those attitudes, beliefs, and self-understandings. The first "type" of evaluation is absolutely essential if Razian legal theory is to be successful in its aims, because a legal theory is explanatorily adequate only if it correctly picks out and explains what is important and significant in the way in which we understand ourselves and our social world in terms of law. Moreover, it might be thought that it is particularly problematic for Raz to drive a wedge between these two "types" of evaluation, because of the point emphasised by both Finnis and Raz that some of the law's important features involve moral claims and attitudes, such as the law's claim that it possesses legitimate moral authority and ought to be obeyed, and the acceptance of that claim by many of those who are subject to the law.

The Finnisian "no place to stop" argument could thus run as follows: it just makes no sense to conceive of two different types of evaluation concerning features of the law, as Raz's position seems to require. No matter if we wish to make special use of the adjective "moral" or not (and, for various reasons, some of which are considered in the next chapter, it might be better to drop it altogether), to evaluate something is to ascribe real value or worth to it, and this univocal meaning is the only one which

---

[33] Raz, "Authority, Law and Morality", in Raz, *Ethics in the Public Domain* (n. 20 *supra*), 236–7. See also Raz, "The Relevance of Coherence" in Raz, *Ethics in the Public Domain*, 300–1, n. 35. This argument of Raz's is examined further in Chapter 6.

the term will bear. We just do not count something as being an evaluation unless it consists of an ascription of such worth, or entails such an ascription. Raz admits that a legal theorist must enter into evaluations of his explanandum in order to construct an adequate account of it, and the only thing which such an evaluation can consist of is: "understanding what is really good for human persons, and what is really required by practical reasonableness".[34]

It is therefore impossible, Finnis might contend, for a legal theorist to do the job which he must do in order for his theory to be explanatorily adequate without himself entering into the business of morally evaluating the law and thereby constructing a theory which depends for its success on correct ascriptions of moral value to features of the law by the theorist concerned.[35] The tenability of Raz's stance—and of the approach to legal theory which it exemplifies—thus depends on being able to meet this challenge successfully. How is it possible for a legal theory to be evaluative in the sense which it must if it is to be explanatorily adequate, without engaging in moral evaluations of its subject matter? This is the puzzle which chapter 3 attempts to solve.

[34] Finnis, *NLNR* (n. 18 *supra*), 1.

[35] This attempt to formulate the kind of challenge which Finnis might want to mount against Raz is heavily influenced by remarks made by Finnis during a seminar which he gave in Oxford in Michaelmas Term, 1994.

3
Indirectly Evaluative Legal Theory: Meeting Finnis' Challenge

The last chapter closed with a statement of a puzzle or problem which, according to Finnis, any legal theorist attempting to hold the methodological position which I have attributed to Raz must face. The puzzle is this: how is it possible for a legal theory to make evaluative judgements about its subject matter in the way which it must in order to be explanatorily adequate, and yet simultaneously to hold that it is not engaging in judgements of the moral merit of features of the law? In this chapter, I introduce and attempt to elucidate a distinction between two different types of evaluative propositions which I believe can come to the aid of a legal theory faced with the kind of gauntlet thrown down by Finnis to Raz in this regard. This distinction is intended to reflect the way that we think about the different kinds of evaluative judgements which we make, and is used in the remainder of this work in order to illuminate and explain important differences in jurisprudential methodology.

A. Directly vs. Indirectly Evaluative Propositions

We can approach the distinction which I have in mind by first of all asking what it is to evaluate something. The obvious answer to this question must be that to evaluate something is to ascribe value or worth to it. If we think, then, of there being some basic category of value, for example, the property of being good, then what I shall refer to as directly evaluative propositions will be those propositions which ascribe value or worth to something in this fundamental sense of accounting it as good. Directly evaluative propositions, then, are those which are of the form, or which entail propositions which are of the form, "X is good".[1] Directly evaluative propositions concerning the law would include: "obedience to law is good"; "there is a general moral obligation to obey the law"; "law necessarily possesses legitimate moral authority over its subjects", and "the law is morally justified". Negative evaluations will not be considered in any detail in terms of this formal definition, or in this work as a whole, although propositions which are of the form, or which entail propositions which are of the form "X is bad" are also directly evaluative propositions (and are mentioned as such on occasion during the following discussion). I focus here mainly upon positive evaluations for the reason that the two theorists whose methodological views I wish to contrast with Raz's, namely Finnis and Dworkin, claim that a legal theory must have recourse to positive directly evaluative propositions concerning the law in order to explain it adequately. For the sake of clarity, however, it should be borne in mind that the points which I make regarding the role of directly evaluative propositions in legal theories apply in respect of both positive and negative directly evaluative propositions.

Directly evaluative propositions, then, are one category or type of evaluative proposition. However, many propositions which we think of as being involved in evaluative work do not fall within this category. One example has already been mentioned in the course of discussing the point that for a legal theory to be explanatorily adequate it must pick out which are the important and significant features of the law to be explained (and must do so in a way which is sufficiently sensitive to the way in which law is already understood by those living under it). To assert that the law's claim that it ought to be obeyed is an important feature of the law which any adequate legal theory will have to explain seems to indicate some evaluative activity on the

[1] If it is the case that there is more than one basic category of value, then the form of this proposition will be the disjunct of all of the basic categories of value, for example "X is good or right or obligatory" etc.

part of one making such an assertion. In this case, however, the main part of the above proposition, which is of the form "X is important" is not itself an ascription of goodness to that X, and nor does it entail a proposition which ascribes goodness to that X. If I contend that the law's claim that it ought to obeyed is an important feature of the law, I have not yet made any judgement to the effect that the law's claim that it ought to obeyed is good or bad, right or wrong, and nor is any such judgement entailed by my contention. All that I have claimed is that X is a feature of the law which, be it good or bad, is of importance and as such requires to be explained.

This being so, we can draw a distinction between the type of propositions wherein such judgements of importance are made, and directly evaluative propositions. The former, which I will term indirectly evaluative propositions, state that a given X has evaluative properties but do not entail directly evaluative propositions stating that this same X is good (or bad). An indirectly evaluative proposition of the form "X is an important feature of the law", is thus a proposition which attributes some evaluative property to that feature of the law, but which does not entail a directly evaluative proposition that the feature of the law in question is good (or bad). Another way of putting this might be to say that in the case of a proposition like "X is an important feature", the evaluation concerned does not go to the substance or content of the subject of the proposition in the same way as is the case with a directly evaluative proposition. In asserting that "X is an important feature", we are accounting the *existence* of some X as significant and hence worthy of explanation, not directly evaluating as good or bad the substance or content of that X. For example, if I claim that leaving his native land was the most important thing that happened to John in his life and is hence important to explain in understanding his life, my claim does not entail that the event in question was a good or bad, wonderful or terrible thing.

Indirectly evaluative propositions such as "X is important", then, state that a given X has evaluative properties but they are evaluative properties from which it does not follow that this same X is good.[2] However, this does not mean to say that there are no other possible relations between directly and indirectly evaluative propositions. For instance, sometimes, a directly evaluative proposition stating that a given X is good may provide support for an indirectly evaluative proposition that this same X is therefore important to explain. An example or two may assist in making this a little clearer. If a certain event was the best thing that ever happened to someone in their life, then it seems clear that this direct evaluation could provide support for the indirectly evaluative proposition that the event in question is important. Such a supporting relation could also hold if the event was the worst thing that ever happened to someone in their life. This, of course, does not threaten the distinction which has been drawn here between the two types of evaluative propositions, because although this example indicates that there can be a supporting relation running *from* directly evaluative propositions *to* indirectly evaluative propositions, still there is no relation of entailment running the other way, i.e. although the fact that a given event was the best (or worst) thing that happened to someone in their life could provide support for a claim that this event is important; stating that a given event is important does not entail that it was the best thing that ever happened in a person's life, nor the worst thing, nor any such directly evaluative proposition in respect of that event.

A judgement that it is important for a legal theory to explain the law's claim to possess legitimate moral authority, and the ascription of such authority to the law on the part of those who accept that claim, would also fall into the indirectly evaluative category. The law invariably claims moral authority over those to whom it is addressed. As will be discussed further below, that this is something which the law always does makes it an important feature of the law to be explained. But

---

[2] There may be types of indirectly evaluative propositions other than those with which I am concerned here, such that analysing this class of propositions may be useful in other areas of philosophy. However, the constraints of the present project dictate that such matters cannot be investigated at the present time.

asserting that the law's invariable claim to possess moral authority is an important feature of the law to be explained does not entail a directly evaluative judgement to the effect that this claim is justified (or unjustified). In making the former indirect evaluation, we are picking out the *existence* of the law's claim as important, not directly evaluating its content. Moreover, and as will also be discussed further below, the law's invariable claim to possess moral authority is important whether this claim is always justified, never justified, rarely justified, justified only under certain conditions, or if it is merely the case that people by and large *think* it is justified, but are largely misguided in so doing.

Where does this leave us in terms of assessing Finnis' and Raz's respective methodological standpoints? The distinction between directly evaluative propositions and indirectly evaluative propositions drawn above is intended to reflect distinctions in the way that we think about the types of evaluative judgements which we make. To the extent that a coherent and tenable such distinction has been drawn, then, it serves in addressing Finnis' point that evaluation is of one kind only, such that when one starts down the evaluative road (as both Finnis and Raz contend that a legal theorist must), there is no place to stop, short of morally evaluating the law in order to understand it adequately. In so doing, the distinction also assists in explaining the way in which Raz can support his legal theory with evaluative judgements that certain features of the law are important to explain without these entailing directly evaluative judgements that the features in question are good things.

It should be clear from the foregoing that propositions which ascribe moral value to the law are included in the category of directly evaluative propositions. However, there may be good reasons for steering away from the term "moral" altogether in conducting the present discussion. First of all, it is not always obvious that the kind of features which make law good or valuable are or should be described as "moral". For example, to claim that good law is capable of expressing and giving effect to the wishes of a community, or that good law is of worth as a set of standards via which we may identify with and perceive ourselves as belonging to a particular community, is to claim that such law is of value, but it may not be immediately clear that this value is one which should be accounted as moral, unless a wide understanding of morality is adopted (as, in fact, I believe that it should be in this context, see further below), such that it is taken as referring to what is good or valuable in life in general, rather than as delineating some narrower category of subject matter as is often the case. Moreover, good law will be valuable in very many ways, some of which will be quite trivial, rendering the term "moral" somewhat incongruous given some of its usual connotations.

In trying to explain the distinction between directly and indirectly evaluative propositions, it may also be wise to avoid the term "moral" for the reason that using this term might give the impression that the difference between direct and indirect evaluation is a difference in the subject matter which is being evaluated: i.e. subject matter which is capable of being designated as moral versus subject matter which cannot be so designated respectively. As I hope the discussion in this chapter makes clear, this would be an erroneous way of understanding the distinction which I am trying to elucidate. Despite these qualms, however, many of the qualities which law can potentially possess are qualities which we think of and refer to as moral qualities, including having legitimate authority and generating a general obligation to obey it, and this is reflected in the terms in which debates within jurisprudence are conducted, and in my own terminology regarding the moral evaluation, moral justification, and beneficial moral consequences theses. This being the case, then, so long as it is borne in mind that in the present context, I intend "moral" to be understood in broad terms, to mean simply that which is good or valuable, then, for the purposes at hand, there is probably little harm in employing the terms direct evaluation and moral evaluation more or less interchangeably (and, indeed, I do so on many occasions throughout the book). This is not to say, however, that there might not be other contexts in which it is wise or indeed necessary to distinguish between them, but I cannot discuss this here.[3]

B. Recasting the Finnisian Challenge

To return to our main topic of discussion: drawing the distinction between directly and indirectly evaluative propositions is intended to assist in parrying Finnis' argument insofar as it comes in the form of a claim that evaluations concerning the law can be of one kind only, such that once we have started down the evaluative road there is no place to stop. However, perhaps Finnis' case against Raz does not rest solely on such a claim. For example, it would still be open to Finnis to contend that, even if we accept the foregoing explanation of the distinction between indirectly and directly evaluative propositions, and accept that the former do not entail the latter, still it is the case that the *only* way in which we can support indirectly evaluative judgements to the effect that a given feature of the law is important, is via direct evaluations regarding whether and to what extent that feature is good or bad.[4] On such a view, legal theorists would still require to engage in direct or moral evaluation in order to make judgements concerning which are the important or significant features of the law to be explained, for the reason that the only way in which those latter type of judgements can be supported is by directly evaluative propositions concerning the features of the law in question. So, for example, Finnis might contend that the reason why the law's claim to moral legitimacy is an important

[3] John Finnis also has some qualms concerning the term "moral" on the grounds that it "is of somewhat uncertain connotation" (J. Finnis, *Natural Law and Natural Rights* (Oxford, Clarendon Press, 1980), 15), and so instead of claiming that a legal theorist must morally evaluate the law, he claims that the theorist must decide for himself what the requirements of practical reasonableness are (see Finnis, *ibid.*, 15–17) in order to understand law properly.

[4] I believe that there are elements of both of these lines of argument in Finnis' position, although, once again, I base this as much on my attempted reconstruction of his views in light of verbal remarks made in Oxford in seminars during the period October 1994–March 1997, as on the text of *Natural Law and Natural Rights* (n. 3 *supra*).

feature of the law to be explained is because law *is* a morally justified phenomenon which lives up to the claims to moral legitimacy which it makes in resolving co-ordination problems for the common good of the community living under it. Direct evaluations concerning the moral legitimacy of the law would thus be driving or providing support for the indirectly evaluative proposition that the law's claim to moral legitimacy is important to explain.

This line of thinking can be rebutted as follows. Although an indirectly evaluative proposition such as that some X is significant and important to explain *can* be supported or justified by directly evaluative propositions concerning that same X (as in my previous example where I claimed that if a given event was the best thing that happened to someone in their life, then this could support the indirectly evaluative proposition that the event was therefore important to explain), still it is not the case that indirectly evaluative propositions can *only* be supported in this way, such that we must take a stance on, for example, whether a given X is good (or bad) in order to know that it is significant and important. Indeed, that indirectly evaluative propositions can be supported in other ways is vital to a proper understanding of the methodological approach to legal theory which I am attempting to elucidate here. This point can best be understood by asking what it is that drives or provides support for judgements that certain features of the law are important to explain in a legal theory such as Raz's.[5]

Legal theory seeks to deepen our understanding of the law. This being the case, in very general terms, the features of the law which are important to explain are those which best reveal the distinctive character of law as a special method of social organisation. For example, in Razian legal theory, one reason why the law's claim to moral authority is important is simply

---

[5] For Raz's views on this issue, see e.g. J. Raz, "Authority, Law and Morality", especially section VI, in J. Raz, *Ethics in the Public Domain* (Oxford, Clarendon Press, 1994); J. Raz, "The Relevance of Coherence" in Raz, *ibid.*, at 295–301; J. Raz, "The Morality of Obedience" (1985) 83 *Michigan Law Review* 732.

because it is something which the law invariably does and which is hence characteristic of it. Moreover, according to Raz, an examination of the nature of this claim will reveal that the law invariably operates in certain distinctive ways, and that it is intended to impinge upon our practical reasoning processes in a particular manner.[6] This being the case, one very general way in which indirectly evaluative propositions that certain features of the law are important to explain may be supported without resort to directly evaluative propositions concerning whether those features are good or bad, is on the basis that they are features which law invariably exhibits, and which hence reveal the distinctive character and mode of operation of the law.

There are other ways, too, of providing support for indirectly evaluative judgements that a given feature of the law is important to explain, without taking a stance on whether or not it is a good or bad thing. In Chapter 2, I emphasised the importance for legal theory of Raz's point that law is a concept which people use to understand themselves. In picking out which features of the law are important to explain, therefore, we must ask what is important as regards the way in which we understand ourselves in terms of the law. This being the case, sometimes a legal theorist may judge that a given feature of the law is important to explain on the basis of the prevalence of certain beliefs concerning that feature on the part of those subject to the law, and the consequences which those beliefs have. Take, once again, the law's claim to possess moral authority. Some of those subject to the law, perhaps especially the officials of a legal system, accept that claim, and that acceptance results in their behaving in certain ways in light of the law. The prevalence of such beliefs, and the effect which those beliefs in the moral authority

---

[6] Namely by creating reasons for action of a certain kind, i.e. reasons which pre-empt certain other reasons for action which someone who is subject to the law might have. See e.g. Raz, "Authority, Law and Morality" in Raz, *Ethics in the Public Domain* (n. 5 *supra*); J. Raz, *The Authority of Law* (Oxford, Clarendon Press, 1979) ch. 1; J. Raz, *The Morality of Freedom* (Oxford, Clarendon Press, 1986), Pt I; J. Raz, *Practical Reason and Norms*, 2nd edn. (Princeton, NJ, Princeton University Press, 1990), *passim*.

of the law have upon the practical orientation of some of those subject to the law renders those beliefs, and the aspect of the law which they concern, important to explain and make intelligible, whether or not the beliefs in question are well-founded.

The point just made mentions the importance of the effects which the law can have upon the practical orientation of those subject to it, and this flags up another way in which indirectly evaluative judgements about features of the law can be supported, namely on the grounds that certain of those features can be adjudged important to explain because they bear upon matters which are of practical concern to us in conducting our lives, given the presence of law. Once again: the law invariably claims moral authority, and hence to lay down standards of right conduct. However, even if the law's claims in this regard are not justified, either in general, or on a particular occasion, still it is the case that the law will treat those falling within its jurisdiction as though those claims are justified. The law will thus treat us as subject to its authority, and will act upon the claims which it makes, for example, by removing or curtailing our freedom in some way if we disobey certain of its edicts. This makes it important to identify and understand what it is about the law, and about the way in which it operates, which makes it capable of having such significant effects upon matters of practical concern to us, irrespective of whether we believe the claims which law makes to be true, whether they really are true, or whether they render law a good or bad thing. In this case too, then, indirect evaluations concerning the importance of certain features of the law need not be supported by direct evaluations concerning whether those features, and the social institution which exhibits them, are good or bad things.

However, perhaps a challenger resistant to the line of thinking I am trying to develop here might want to point out that, in this case, the reason why these practical effects which the law can have upon our lives are important to us is because we value the freedom and autonomy which they threaten to remove or curtail. Various direct evaluations concerning the nature of freedom and autonomy, and regarding the conditions under which we do and should hold such notions to be valuable, are thus part of the background which make those aspects of legal regulation which threaten to impinge upon them of practical concern to us and hence important to explain. Does this not demand, then, our challenger might continue, that legal theorists must undertake direct evaluations regarding, for example, the nature of freedom and autonomy, whether and under what conditions the law is justified in impinging upon them, and hence whether and under what conditions the law is a good or a bad thing, in order to know which features of it are important to explain?

The approach to legal theory propounded here claims that the challenger's question can be answered in the negative. Although this challenge hints at an important connection between certain directly evaluative judgements, and indirect evaluations to the effect that certain features of the law are important to explain, still it is not the case that those judgements of importance need be supported by directly evaluative judgements regarding those features or the social institution which exhibits them. What the above challenge should alert us to is the possibility that sometimes, what is driving the importance of a certain feature of the law is the fact that understanding the nature of the feature in question has a bearing upon, or is ultimately relevant to, answering directly evaluative questions regarding the law and its relation to certain values. To put the matter another way: sometimes, the reason why a given feature of the law *is* important to explain is because understanding the nature of that feature is vitally important when we go on to consider questions such as what we ought to do in light of it, and in light of the social institution which exhibits it. However, we can often know that a certain feature of the law has a bearing upon or is relevant to eventually answering questions such as whether law is a good or bad, justified or unjustified social institution, and hence what we ought to do, given the presence of law, without yet having to take a stance upon the answers to those questions. Indeed, we may go further, and say that we cannot properly begin to answer a question such as: "what ought we to do, given the presence of law?" until we know what law is like, and which distinctive considerations its presence brings to bear upon our practical reasoning processes. In explaining his own view of correct jurisprudential methodology, Raz gives the following example which may assist in illustrating these points:

> "A theory of what the law is strives to identify its central, prominent, important features. What makes a feature prominent or important or central is inescapably and inevitably an evaluative question. It is important if it bears upon what matters. In large measure it is precisely the fact that certain features are relevant to what one ought to do which marks their importance.
>
> It is crucial to remember, however, that we can and often do know that a feature of a scheme or institution is relevant to its evaluation without knowing whether that makes it good or bad. The fact that primary education is compulsory is recognised by all as important to its evaluation, regardless of whether they take it to be one of the strengths or rather weaknesses of our educational arrangements".[7]

Likewise, the law's claim to moral authority is important because the nature of this claim means that the law will hold us to certain standards whether we like it or not, and is a force which is capable of impinging upon our lives in certain distinctive ways. Moreover, the ways in which it does impinge upon our lives, namely by claiming to state what we really ought to do, and removing or curtailing our freedom if we fail to comply with it, means that it has a bearing upon and is relevant to directly evaluative questions such as whether and under what conditions the law is a good or a bad thing, and, given the answers to those questions, whether and under what conditions we ought to obey it. The point which Raz seeks to emphasise in the passages just quoted is that it is possible to know this—to know that certain of the ways in which the law operates will be *relevant* to any eventual moral or direct evaluation of it—without having to make those directly evaluative judgements. Whether one espouses the view that the law is always justified in the claims to moral authority which it makes, a Razian view that

---

[7] Raz, "The Morality of Obedience" (n. 5 *supra*), 735.

it is sometimes, and under certain conditions so justified,[8] or an anarchist view that the law is never justified in any of the claims it makes, all can agree that law's important features include its distinctive mode of operation, and the manner in which, via its claim to moral authority, it holds us to certain standards and hence has a bearing upon matters of practical concern to us. Moreover, all can agree that the ways in which law operates—for example, that it purports to tell us what we really ought to do and acts against us by removing or curtailing our freedom if we fail to comply with it—render certain features of the law relevant to whatever direct evaluations we eventually might wish to make regarding whether those features, and the social institution which exhibits them, are good or bad, justified or unjustified and hence what we ought to do in light of this. This being the case, the distinction between indirectly evaluative and directly evaluative propositions can assist in emphasising the way in which judgements regarding the importance or significance of certain features of the law do not yet involve, although they may be an important precursor to, direct evaluations of the law.

The above remarks thus indicate another force which drives the importance of certain features of the law in the indirectly evaluative approach to legal theory. Although we often do not know, and do not have to take a stance upon, whether certain features of the law are good or bad things, we can know that those features are relevant to any such eventual assessments, and that, for this reason, it is important to understand and explain them.[9] To come at the matter from another angle, we might even say that once indirectly evaluative legal theory has done its job of laying bare and explaining those important features of the law, it is then possible and appropriate to go on and make directly evaluative judgements concerning whether those

[8] See J. Raz, *The Morality of Freedom* (n. 6 *supra*), Pt I; Raz, "Authority, Law and Morality" in Raz, *Ethics in the Public Domain* (n. 5 *supra*).

[9] Wil Waluchow draws attention to this mode of supporting indirect evaluations of the importance of certain features of the law in W. Waluchow, *Inclusive Legal Positivism* (Oxford, Clarendon Press, 1994), 19–29.

features, and the social institution which exhibits them, are good or bad.[10]

To sum up: contrary to the line of reasoning which, albeit not in the terminology used here, can be discerned in Finnis' position, an indirectly evaluative proposition such as "X is important" does not entail a directly evaluative proposition that this same X is good. Furthermore, although a proposition in the form "X is important" may be supported by a directly evaluative judgement that this same X is good, this is not the *only* means by which such a proposition can be supported, and, indeed, that there are other ways in which indirectly evaluative propositions may be supported is vitally important in understanding the approach to legal theory which I am using Raz's position to illuminate. According to that approach, indirectly evaluative propositions which state that some feature of the law, X, is important to explain may also be supported by the fact that X is a feature which law invariably exhibits, and which hence reveals the distinctive mode of law's operation; by the prevalence and consequences of certain beliefs on the part of those subject to law concerning X, indicating its centrality to our self-understandings; by the fact that the X in question bears upon matters of practical concern to us; and/or by the way in which X is relevant to or has a bearing upon various directly evaluative questions concerning whether it and the social institution which exhibits it are good or bad things. In this book, I seek to draw attention to and explain the sense in which the indirectly evaluative propositions to which any explanatorily adequate legal theory must have recourse can be supported in one or more of the ways just listed, i.e. otherwise than on the basis of directly evaluative propositions concerning features of the law. Moreover, I also want to advocate that proceeding in this way represents the correct methodological approach for a theory of law to adopt. The reasons behind this, which begin to emerge in the discussions in Chapters 6 and 7, ultimately lie with the type of data

[10] I discuss this aspect of the relation between direct and indirect evaluation further in the book's concluding chapter.

with which legal theory is concerned, which is such that indirectly evaluative propositions about features of the law can be supported other than via directly evaluative propositions about the law (as the foregoing discussion also indicates), and with the point that proceeding in this way allows us to explain and understand certain features of the law without prejudging the issue of whether they render the law a good or a bad thing.[11]

C. Directly vs. Indirectly Evaluative Legal Theory

In this chapter, I have attempted to draw a distinction between directly and indirectly evaluative propositions. In the present context, however, we are primarily concerned not with the nature of propositions but with the nature of theories. A directly evaluative theory, then, will be a theory which contains at least one proposition which is a directly evaluative proposition concerning features of the law (or which contains at least one proposition which entails a directly evaluative proposition concerning features of the law). Finnis' approach to theorising about law is thus such a theory. His account contains directly evaluative propositions which make judgements about the goodness of the law and the moral obligations which it creates, in the course of identifying and explaining law's important features.

According to Finnis, such judgements are necessary in order for a legal theory to be explanatorily adequate. Raz disagrees, in the sense that he rejects the moral evaluation thesis and does not believe that it is necessary for legal theories to contain directly evaluative propositions concerning those features of the law which we judge to be important or significant to explain. In order for Raz's legal theory to be explanatorily adequate,

[11] It should be remembered, however, that owing to the point raised in section B of Chapter 1 concerning the likely interrelation between methodologies and the substantive theories of law which they support, I do not pretend to offer a conclusive argument in favour of the indirectly evaluative approach to legal theory in this work. In large part, my task is to deepen our understanding of this approach, and to show how some of those espousing rival methodological positions have been mistaken in assuming that there is no ground for it to occupy.

however, it must pick out and explain the important and significant features of law, and, moreover, must do so in ways which reflect what those subject to the law regard as important about it, including, where they have them, their views concerning the law's moral status. The theory will thus contain, or be supported by,[12] indirectly evaluative propositions concerning various features of the law. Finnis claims that a legal theory cannot be explanatorily adequate without making directly evaluative judgements about those important features of the law. This claim issues either from (a) the view that there is and can be only one type of evaluation, or that indirectly evaluative propositions entail directly evaluative propositions, such that when one begins to make evaluative judgements concerning the law there is no place to stop, or from (b) the thesis that indirectly evaluative propositions about features of the law can *only* be supported by directly evaluative propositions concerning those features. However, if, as has been claimed in the foregoing discussion: (1) we can draw a coherent and tenable distinction between indirectly evaluative propositions and directly evaluative propositions, in order to emphasise that "X is important" does not entail that this same X is good, and (2) we can explain the way in which a judgement that X is important in the case of some feature of the law can be supported otherwise than on the basis of direct evaluations concerning X, then Finnis' point, in whichever form he would choose to make it, need not hold. It will thus be possible for Raz to have what I propose to term an indirectly evaluative theory of law, i.e. an account of law which is supported by indirectly evaluative propositions concerning the importance and significance of certain features of the law, but

---

[12] I formulate things this way because while some theories will explicitly contain within themselves propositions which state that the reason why a given feature of the law is being explained is because of its importance or significance in understanding the social institution of law, others will not contain such explicit meta-theoretical propositions and will instead be implicitly supported by indirectly evaluative propositions (and would become explicitly so if, for example, we were to challenge the theorist as to why he has focused on a particular feature of law in his account).

which does not itself have to enter into the business of making directly evaluative judgements concerning whether those features, and the social institution which exhibits them, are good or bad, justified or unjustified.

We are now in a better position to grasp why, at the beginning of Chapter 2, I objected to the descriptive/normative and value-free/value-laden dichotomies, and to the way in which they are employed by some commentators on this topic. Indirectly evaluative legal theory involves evaluative judgements about features of the law to an extent which I hope makes it quite clear why "value-free" is a totally inaccurate characterisation of such an approach, and why "descriptive" is misleading at best. Nevertheless, this approach to legal theory is most certainly not "normative" if that is understood to mean that the theory must involve direct or moral evaluations of the law in order to pick out and explain its important features. Rather, the indirectly evaluative approach involves evaluative judgements regarding which are the important and significant features of the law to be explained, in the sense, and for the reasons, which I have tried to illuminate in this discussion.

D. Law's Aspirations

The discussion so far should have brought the nature of the methodological dispute between Finnis and Raz more clearly into focus, and helped to introduce the indirectly evaluative approach to legal theory. *Contra* Finnis, Raz's view is that a successful legal theory need not contain directly evaluative propositions concerning features of the law. However, it would be a mistake to think that this means that Raz, and the indirectly evaluative approach to legal theory of which I have claimed he is a proponent, is less interested than Finnis in investigating questions concerning the aspirations and ideals which the social institution of law should live up to. As the foregoing discussion should have already made clear, a theory such as Raz's does hold that understanding the ideals to which law aspires is important in explaining its nature:

"the law claims to have legitimate moral authority. This explains why the law is presented in moral terms . . . The significance of the shared terminology . . . does not attest to what law is but to what it aspires to be. It is an expression of the fact that the law necessarily claims legitimate authority. It follows, of course, that where a legal system is in force many, most notably its officials, believe that claim to be justified. What does not follow is that it is justified. Still the fact is crucial to the understanding of the sort of institution the law is and—from the moral point of view—it sets the standards by which the law is to be judged".[13]

For Raz, then, understanding the claims which law makes and the ideals to which it aspires is very much part of understanding the nature of law. The important point to be grasped, however, is that indirectly evaluative legal theory contends that in order to achieve that understanding, it is not necessary to undertake moral or direct evaluation of aspects of the law.[14] To come at this matter by way of analogy: imagine an agnostic observer who wants to understand a Roman Catholic mass which he attends. In order to be successful in his task, this observer will obviously have to engage in evaluative work, for in order to understand the mass, he will have to understand, amongst other things, what it is for mass to be celebrated well. This will require an evaluation of which things it is important for various of the involved parties to do correctly and an understanding of what those actions mean for them. The observer will, therefore, inevitably be making judgements about which are the most important or significant features of the mass, and which ideals a well-celebrated mass should live up to. However, the observer's judgement that a particular feature of the mass is important or significant will not be supported by his own direct evaluations regarding whether that feature or the ideals to which it is alleged to contribute are good or bad, right or wrong—he is agnostic as regards these matters and is not in the business of making any such evaluations. Rather, the observer's indirectly evaluative

---

[13] J. Raz, "On the Nature of Law" (1996) 82 *Archive für Rechts und Sozialphilosophie* 1–25, at 16.

[14] The idea that the claims which law makes set the standards by which it is to be judged from the moral point of view is briefly revisited in Chapter 7.

judgements of the importance of a given feature of the mass will be supported or justified by the role which that feature plays in the self-understandings of those participants in the mass. Those self-understandings will include the attribution of spiritual and moral value in respect of certain aspects of the mass, and those attributions of value indicate the things which matter to participants in the mass and which are thus important to explain. However, according to the approach which I am attempting to elucidate here, the agnostic observer need not share those values, nor himself take a stance on whether the participants are correct in their ascriptions of spiritual and moral value, in order to understand which features of the mass are important and significant for those participating in it.[15]

In the same way, even an anarchist harbouring wholehearted moral disapproval of the very idea of legal regulation may understand what a legal system is trying to do, the necessary features which it must have in order to do that (including, for example, the claims to moral authority which it makes and the acceptance by some of those claims), the ideals to which it aspires (although he will obviously not regard them as truly being ideals), and the way in which it may fail to live up to those ideals. In order to attain such understanding, the anarchist will have to be able to identify and adequately explain the most important and significant features of this social institution, including, once again, features which involve moral claims, and the ascription of moral value, such as the law's claim to be morally legitimate and the acceptance by some of that claim. By drawing attention to the fact that indirectly evaluative propositions about features of the law do not entail their directly evaluative counterparts, and indicating how the former can be supported other than by way of those directly evaluative counterparts, I have tried to provide a framework which explains how the anarchist could construct a successful legal theory without taking a stance on the moral value of such features of the law.

[15] This point is offered merely as an analogy which might assist in illuminating the manner in which indirectly evaluative legal theory proceeds.

4
Finnis and the Moral Justification Thesis

The preceding two chapters have been concerned with the first of the three methodological issues which this work addresses, namely whether it is necessary to morally evaluate the law in order to understand it adequately. In this chapter, however, I turn, albeit much more briefly, to our second issue, namely the moral justification thesis. The question to be addressed, then, is whether a legal theory need hold the law to be morally justified in order to understand it adequately.

A. From Evaluation to Justification

In Chapter 2 (section C), I claimed that Finnis' position is distinguished from Raz's by two theses which the former supports and the latter rejects, namely: (1) in order to evaluate which are law's important features, and to explain those features, the legal theorist must morally evaluate the law, and (2) that such an evaluation will lead to the conclusion that the law is a morally justified phenomenon which lives up to its claims that it is morally authoritative and ought to be obeyed.

Finnis' support for the second of the above theses is, like his support for the first, apparent from the opening chapter of *Natural Law and Natural Rights*.[1] Indeed, in that chapter, he does not seem to distinguish between the moral evaluation and moral justification theses, so that once he has argued that legal theories require recourse to moral evaluation, in the sense that

[1] See J. Finnis, *Natural Law and Natural Rights* (Oxford, Clarendon Press, 1980) (hereinafter *NLNR*), *passim*, but especially 14–17.

in order to pick out and explain the important features of law, the legal theorist must take a stance on, "what the requirements of practical reasonableness really are",[2] and on the role of law with regard to those requirements, Finnis appears to assume that any theorist so doing will come to the conclusion that law should be understood as a morally justified phenomenon as well.

As was mentioned in Chapter 2, Finnis contends that the proper way to understand law is to attempt to elucidate the focal meaning or central case of the phenomenon in question.[3] In order to do this, he claims, legal theorists must not merely pick out as important and give an adequate account of the various possible attitudes towards the law exhibited by those who are subject to it, including the attitude that the law's claim to authority is true. Rather, those theorists must take a stance on which attitude toward the law it is correct to adopt, and use it as their standard of reference in characterising law. According to Finnis, the attitude in question is that of someone who believes that law is morally justified in the claims, including the claim that it ought to be obeyed, which it makes:

> "If there is a point of view in which legal obligation is treated as at least presumptively a moral obligation . . . then such a viewpoint will constitute the central case of the legal viewpoint . . . such a viewpoint is the viewpoint which should be used as the standard of reference by the theorist describing the features of the legal order".[4]

For Finnis, then, the methodological stance which the legal theorist must take in order to understand law adequately will result in his theory holding the law to be morally justified. As the above quotation should make clear, in Finnis' account, to say that a legal theorist must hold the law to be morally justified in order to understand it adequately is to say that the theorist must characterise the law from the point of view of one who holds it to be justified in the claims which it makes, including the claims

[2] Finnis, *NLNR* (n. 1 *supra*), 16.
[3] See Chapter 2, section C.
[4] Finnis, *NLNR* (n. 1 *supra*), 14–15.

that it has moral authority and generates a general moral obligation to obey it.

In Chapter 1 of *Natural Law and Natural Rights*, then, Finnis appears to move seamlessly from the moral evaluation to the moral justification thesis, perhaps believing that they are one and the same, or that the case which he makes in favour of the former will suffice for the latter as well.[5] However, the assumption that the moral justification thesis must follow from the moral evaluation thesis can be challenged as follows.[6] Even if we were to accept that: (1) it is necessary for a legal theory to morally evaluate the law in order to explain its nature, this is not enough of itself to take us all the way to thesis (2) which further claims that the evaluation concerned will lead to the conclusion that the law is morally justified and ought to be obeyed. Thesis (1) states only that a legal theorist must take *some* stance on the moral value of the law in order to understand it adequately. Even if we interpret this as requiring that in order to understand law adequately, a legal theorist needs to take a stance on the conditions under which law would be morally justified, there is still a significant gap between this claim, and the further claim that law *is* a morally justified social institution whose claims that it ought to be obeyed are true. Thesis (1), for example, is a methodological precept which could be accepted by a critical race theorist who believes that in many instances, law operates in a way which results in great injustice to persons of colour. Such a theorist could well hold that in order to have an adequate account of law, it is always necessary to morally evaluate the law, and perhaps even take a stance on the conditions under which law would be morally justified and on whether a particular instance of law is

[5] In my view, Finnis does not tell us enough about the structure of his argument or differentiate the two theses sufficiently to enable this matter to be settled decisively. It is of course my contention that the points made in this chapter regarding the relation between the two theses still hold, irrespective of what Finnis' view of the matter may be.

[6] My thinking as regards some of the following points was influenced by issues which were discussed during the course of a seminar given by Joseph Raz in Columbia Law School, New York, in the Fall Semester of 1995.

in fact morally justified, but would certainly not contend, as Finnis does, that the central case of law is a morally justified institution. In fact, it would be open to a critical race theorist both to hold that in order to understand law adequately we must morally evaluate it, and to contend that it is in the nature of law that it operates in such morally reprehensible ways in respect of its dealings with persons of colour that its claims that it ought to be obeyed are never justified.

If confronted with this point, however, I suspect that Finnis might claim that I am mischaracterising his position in ascribing to him the view that it is in the nature of law that it is morally justified, such as to rule out the possibility of a legal theorist concluding that many or indeed all instances of law are not morally justified and ought not be obeyed. My reasons for this suspicion lies with passages such as the following, where Finnis may appear not to be claiming that it is in the nature of law that it is a morally justified phenomenon:

> "It is the object of this book . . . to show how and on what conditions such institutions [of human law] are justified and the ways in which they can be (and often are) defective" . . .[7]

> The intention has not been to describe existing social orders . . . Above all, the meaning has been constructed as a *focal* meaning, not as an appropriation of the term 'law' in a univocal sense that would exclude from the reference of the term anything that failed to have all the characteristics . . . of the central case".[8]

These passages may suggest that Finnis does not wish to exclude morally defective examples of legal regulation from the ambit of law. Such instances will be "law" in one sense, just not in the focal sense which Finnis seeks to elucidate throughout *Natural Law and Natural Rights*. This strand in Finnis' thinking is, of course, part of his attempt to distance himself, and the Thomist natural law tradition from which he regards himself as hailing, from the *lex injusta non est lex* (an unjust law is not a law) doctrine, or, more precisely, from some of the problematic

---

[7] Finnis, *NLNR* (n. 1 *supra*), 3.

[8] Finnis, *NLNR* (n. 1 *supra*), 277.

consequences which some contemporary critics of natural law thinking have assumed must follow from this doctrine.[9] To this end, Finnis claims that his theory is compatible with some of the tenets of legal positivism, and, in particular, that it can incorporate some version of legal positivism's social thesis as regards the identification of legal rules in what he calls an "intra-systemic sense".[10]

It is my view that there are some difficulties with Finnis' stance in this regard. For example, it is important to note that his position is only compatible with the social thesis because of the constantly shifting way in which he uses the term "law". For Finnis, it is possible for a norm to meet the intra-systemic criteria necessary to account it as law in one sense, for example, as a result of being properly enacted by the relevant legislature, whilst simultaneously failing to be a good example of the central case or focal meaning of the social institution of law which he characterises throughout the course of *Natural Law and Natural Rights*. This latter takes us well beyond the social facts with which positivism's social thesis is concerned, because, for Finnis, the central case or focal meaning of law consists of:

> "rules made, in accordance with regulative legal rules . . . for a 'complete' community...this ensemble of rules and institutions being directed to reasonably resolving any of the community's co-ordination problems . . . for the common good of that community, according to a manner and form itself adapted to that common good . . .".[11]

Jurisprudential discussions abound with examples of laws which, to put the matter in Finnisian terms, meet the "intrasystemic" test, but fall down quite radically on the "promulgated

[9] See Finnis, *NLNR* (n. 1 *supra*), 363–6.

[10] Finnis, *NLNR* (n. 1 *supra*), 357. The social thesis claims that what is law and what is not is a matter of social fact. See also *NLNR*, 268: "The primary legal method of showing that a rule is valid is to show (i) that there was at some past time, $t1$, an act (of a legislator, court, or other appropriate institution) which according to the rules in force at $t1$ amounted to a valid and therefore operative act of rule-creation, and (ii) that since $t1$ the rule thus created has not determined (ceased to be in force)".

[11] Finnis, *NLNR* (n. 1 *supra*), 276.

for the common good and hence morally justified/creating a moral obligation to obey them" criterion. For instance, that perennial jurisprudential chestnut, "Nazi law", and many of the laws of South Africa's apartheid regime would seem to fall into this category. With regard to such laws, Finnis must employ the term "law" in two different senses, as wants to claim that they are laws in one sense, but not in another.[12]

The ends which such shifts in meaning can serve become apparent when we consider a point which is of great significance here, namely that Finnis also wants to claim that there is a general moral obligation to obey the law, or that the law is morally justified in the claims, including the claim to be obeyed, which it makes.[13] This point can only stand, however, when Finnis' is using "law" in the second (focal meaning), and not the first (purely intra-systemic) sense. This invites the question of whether Finnis' account can, after all, really be compatible with legal positivism's social thesis. For example, is law which offends against the common good and so does not bring with it a moral obligation to obey, but which does meet the relevant intra-systemic tests, law or not? Surely the answer matters. Legal positivism has an answer; Finnis has what might be viewed as a sleight of hand—it is law in one sense and yet not in another—which he believes allows him both to subscribe to the social thesis, and to claim that it is in the focal meaning of law that it is a morally justified phenomenon.

In response to this point, I believe that Finnis might well agree with at least part of my diagnosis, but strongly deny that any kind of cure is necessary. Rather, he would claim that there is no difficulty with using "law" in two different senses, and that it is unproblematic to move between them in the way just indicated.[14] Moreover, for Finnis, it is not merely a matter of flipping between two clearly demarcated concepts of "law"—law in the focal sense which is morally justified and carries with it a moral obligation to obey it, and law in the peripheral sense

[12] See Finnis, *NLNR* (n. 1 *supra*), chs X to XII. See in particular 354–66.
[13] See Finnis, *NLNR* (n. 1 *supra*), 357–61.
[14] See e.g. Finnis, *NLNR* (n. 1 *supra*), 363–6.

which passes some kind of social facts test, but which is also unjust such that it fails to generate a moral obligation to obey it—for Finnis in fact holds that legality is a matter of degree, "lawness" being something which should be understood on the model of a gas-tap or dimmer switch rather than an on/off light switch.[15] This being so, Finnis would contend, there is neither need nor point in "biting the bullet" and deciding where to draw the line around what is law, leaving what is not outside.

Although I cannot conduct a detailed discussion of this aspect of Finnis' position at the present time, I will attempt to indicate the general tenor of my views with regard to it, in the hope that this will help to shed some light upon the conclusions which follow. I regard Finnis' "degrees of law" thesis as problematic for the reason that it does not seem to take seriously the enterprise of identifying what law's essential properties are. Moreover, it does not seem to take this enterprise as seriously as Finnis himself evidently takes it all the way through *Natural Law and Natural Rights*. Surely it matters to Finnis whether or not law is the kind of social institution which generates a general moral obligation to obey it? This is an issue which Finnis foregrounds in his book and which he tries throughout to convince us lies right at the heart of understanding what law is, and the values which it can help us to realise in our lives. Whether or not it is in the nature of law that it creates a general moral obligation to obey it is thus evidently an important question which Finnis commits himself to answering in the course of *Natural Law and Natural Rights*, and answer it he does, in the affirmative.[16] Having done so, and having so unswervingly argued a case to this effect, it seems odd that he then also wishes to espouse the view that we can say of a norm which passes the relevant social facts test but which offends against the common good and so does not bring with it an obligation to obey it, either that it is

[15] Finnis, *NLNR* (n. 1 *supra*), 276–81.

[16] On the indirectly evaluative approach to understanding law this can also be regarded an important question, but it is one which should be postponed until many other questions about the nature of law have been answered. See further pp. 60–64 *supra* and the discussion in Chapter 7, section A.

law, or that it is not law, and that there is no need to take a decisive stance on what law's essential properties are.

For those who find themselves in sympathy with Finnis' views on this matter, the brief discussion of them offered in this chapter will seem all too unsatisfactory. My plea in mitigation is that the present project is not an exploration of the work of John Finnis, and so discusses his views only to the extent necessary to illuminate those methodological matters currently under consideration. This being so, I undertook the foregoing detour largely in order to make it clear that I am aware that there are many issues concerning Finnis' idea of a focal meaning or central case analysis, and his shifting use of the term "law", but that, nonetheless, I regard the following points as still holding: (1) for Finnis, the central case of law, or law in the focal sense is a morally justified phenomenon which creates a general moral obligation to obey it; (2) in *Natural Law and Natural Rights*, this first point is presented as following from Finnis' arguments to the effect that it is necessary to morally evaluate the law in order to understand it adequately; (3) as I understand his position, it is the central case or focal meaning of law which Finnis attempts to elucidate throughout *Natural Law and Natural Rights*, and it is thus the essential features of this phenomenon which Finnis is trying to capture in his work; and, (4) this being, so, for Finnis, the legal theorist who wishes to understand the nature of law must necessarily morally evaluate the law, and understand it as a morally justified phenomenon which generates a moral obligation to obey it in order to comprehend it properly.

B. Supporting the Moral Justification Thesis by Other Means

With these remarks in mind we can return to the main point under discussion in this chapter. I have attempted to challenge Finnis' apparent assumption that it follows from the thesis that it is necessary to morally evaluate the law in order to understand it adequately (the moral evaluation thesis), that the social institution of law is properly understood as being morally justified such that it ought to be obeyed (the moral justification thesis). The moral evaluation thesis could be espoused by a critical race theorist, a Marxist legal theorist, or even an anarchist, any of whom might well claim that we must return some moral judgement on the law in order to understand it adequately, but also contend that it is in the nature of law that it is a morally reprehensible phenomenon, or at least that there are many instances of law which are unjust and ought not to be obeyed. This being so, I have claimed, Finnis' moral justification thesis is distinct from the moral evaluation thesis, and must be established by independent argument. Whether or not Finnis himself recognises that this is necessary, some such independent argument is in fact present in his position, and comes in two forms: an argument concerning the function of law on the one hand, and a claim about the correct point of view for a legal theorist to adopt on the other.

Regarding the first: Finnis bases his claim that it is in the nature of law that it is morally justified on what I shall term his "unanimity/legal authority gambit".[17] As the plot of *Natural Law and Natural Rights* unfolds, Finnis moves from certain theses regarding what he refers to as the basic goods and requirements of practical reasonableness,[18] to the claim that a legal system is the only way in which we can instantiate such goods in our lives. He does so via the contention that the co-ordination problems to which any society will necessarily be subject in the course of attempts by its members to secure the basic goods can only be solved in one of two ways: by unanimous agreement, or by the authority provided by the law. The former dismissed as a utopian impossibility, it is law's status as the *only* medium via which such co-ordination problems may be solved which justifies the claims that it is morally authoritative and ought to be obeyed, which it makes.[19] In other words, law is morally

[17] See Finnis, *NLNR* (n. 1 *supra*), ch. IX.

[18] Finnis, *NLNR* (n. 1 *supra*), chs III to V.

[19] For a critical assessment of this aspect of Finnis' work, see L. Green, "Law, Co-ordination, and the Common Good" (1983), 3 *Oxford Journal of Legal Studies* 299–324.

justified because it is the only means by which we can realise the basic goods in our lives, and as such, it is better than nothing/an improvement on how things would be without it.

The point of view argument on the other hand, elaborates upon Finnis' commitment to the moral evaluation thesis—that it is necessary to morally evaluate the law in order to understand it—by further claiming that legal theorists will not achieve the requisite understanding unless they understand, themselves take a stance on, and having correctly determined it, adopt, the point of view or attitude towards the law of the truly practically reasonable man. This results in Finnis' position attempting to push the moral evaluation thesis all the way to the moral justification thesis because, according to Finnis: (a) the practically reasonable man is the man with the correct moral views as regards understanding the law, and (b) those views include holding that the law is justified in its claims that it is morally authoritative and ought to be obeyed.[20]

The foregoing remarks are intended to assist in illuminating the moral justification thesis, its relation to the moral evaluation thesis, and the arguments in favour of the former which Finnis provides us with. Once again, a more in-depth examination of these themes cannot be undertaken here, and because of this, the points made below are not intended as conclusive arguments against Finnis' stance in this regard. Insofar as I have any critical comment to make, then, it comes merely in the form of a reminder that Finnis' arguments for pushing the moral evaluation thesis all the way to the moral justification thesis are going to have to do a lot of work in order to be successful, due to the strength of the conclusion which they are required to substantiate. The important point to note is that Finnis is attempting to establish much more than that every legal system, of necessity, must have at least some moral *merit*, a claim which it seems possible an argument like his unanimity/legal authority gambit about the function of law could potentially establish. This

[20] The discussion in Chapter 3 was, of course, intended to cast doubt upon Finnis' claim that in order to characterise law adequately we must understand it as his practically reasonable man understands it.

perhaps quite plausible claim would, however, be compatible with the view that in many instances, the legal system in question also perpetrates such a great deal of evil that its claim that it is morally authoritative and ought to be obeyed is simply false. The further conclusion which Finnis needs the above arguments to establish is that it is in the nature of legal systems that they are morally *justified*, i.e. correct in the claims to moral authority and in the demands to be obeyed on their own terms which they make. This conclusion is very strong, and in need of a suitably powerful argument in its favour. As I claimed previously, such an argument must be independent of Finnis' submissions in favour of the moral evaluation thesis, because the moral justification thesis does not follow automatically from it. The moral evaluation and moral justification theses are distinct positions, such that, for example, a critical race theorist could espouse the former but reject the latter. This being so, it is my contention that Finnis' moral justification thesis does not follow from his arguments in favour of the moral evaluation thesis in the way in which he appears to assume, and, I would suggest, cannot easily be established by mustering arguments employed elsewhere in *Natural Law and Natural Rights* either.

5
The Beneficial Moral Consequences Thesis and an Introduction to Dworkinian Methodology

As I indicated in the overview provided at the end of Chapter 1,[1] the present chapter forms a kind of bridge in the book, between Finnis' challenge to the indirectly evaluative approach to legal theory discussed in Chapters 2 to 4, and Dworkin's challenge to that approach which is examined in the next chapter. Having considered the first two of the three issues into which I initially separated the question, "can you have an adequate account of law 'as it is' which is distinct from an account of how it ought to be?"—i.e. the moral evaluation and moral justification theses—in the context of the Finnis-Raz debate, the present chapter deals with the third of those issues, namely the beneficial moral consequences thesis. The issue now under examination, then, is whether value judgements concerning the beneficial moral consequences of espousing a certain theory of law may legitimately feature in the criteria of success of legal theories. To recap: the reasons for dealing with this issue within this bridging chapter, and before returning to an examination of the moral evaluation and moral justification theses in relation to Dworkin's position, are two-fold. First of all, the beneficial moral consequences thesis is sometimes confused with the first of the three main issues which the book addresses, namely whether a legal theorist need morally evaluate the law in order to understand it

[1] See Chapter 1, section D.

adequately. This being the case, I believe that the contrast between the two issues can best be brought out by first discussing the moral evaluation thesis, and then introducing and explaining the beneficial moral consequences thesis immediately thereafter. Secondly, one of the main arguments which I discuss in considering the beneficial moral consequences thesis provides a useful lead-in to Dworkin's position.

I begin, then, by discussing one version of the beneficial moral consequences thesis and offering some critical comment on it. Following this, I introduce Dworkin's methodological position, and consider whether there are traces of a similar sort of beneficial moral consequences argument within it. Having answered this question in the negative, this chapter leaves the scene set for the one which follows it, in which I return to the moral evaluation and moral justification theses, and to the nature of indirectly evaluative legal theory, this time considering these matters in relation to Dworkin's views.

A. Evaluation and Identification: Schauer's Argument from Beneficial Moral Consequences

Can value judgements concerning the beneficial moral consequences of espousing a certain theory of law legitimately feature in the criteria of success of legal theories? Some of the points raised by Frederick Schauer in his article, "Positivism as Pariah"[2] indicate that he would answer this question in the affirmative.

In this article, Schauer seeks to defend legal positivism from certain charges which are sometimes made against it; for example, that this way of understanding law facilitates complicity with immoral laws on the part of legal officials, or, at the very least, that legal positivism has more morally deleterious consequences as regards this issue than do its natural law or other anti-

[2] F. Schauer, "Positivism as Pariah" in R.P. George (ed.), *The Autonomy of Law: Essays on Legal Positivism* (Oxford, Clarendon Press, 1996) (hereinafter "Positivism as Pariah", with all references being given according to the pagination in *The Autonomy of Law*).

positivist rivals. As Schauer documents, such charges are apparently made on the basis that, because legal positivism does not require legal officials to subject the law to critical moral scrutiny in order to identify what it is, this approach thereby also facilitates the unthinking and uncritical official application of the law, irrespective of its immoral nature or consequences.[3]

As it stands, this claim is open to the charge that it involves a *non sequitur*, stemming from the failure to separate the question of how the law is to be identified, from the quite separate matter of whether or not it should be applied (or, from the point of view not of officials, but of those subject to it, obeyed), a separation which the legal positivist tradition quite clearly recognises.[4] Schauer, too, maintains that the above charges against legal positivism are false, and that they rest upon a misconception of that approach to understanding law. While I certainly concur with this conclusion, I nonetheless wish to highlight some difficulties with the moves which Schauer makes in the course of his exoneration of the positivist enterprise, difficulties which have a bearing upon the present discussion of the beneficial moral consequences thesis.

One plank in Schauer's argument is his claim that legal positivism, far from encouraging the unthinking acceptance of the law, in fact promotes subjecting it to critical moral scrutiny. The alleged reason for this lies with what is often referred to as the social thesis, i.e. legal positivism's claim that what counts as law in a particular jurisdiction ultimately turns on matters of social fact.[5] Schauer claims that because, according to the social

[3] Schauer, "Positivism as Pariah" (n. 2 *supra*), 35. Schauer mentions Gustav Radbruch, Lon Fuller, Robert Cover and Pierre Schlag as being amongst legal positivism's accusers in this regard. See Schauer, *ibid.*, nn. 7–10 at 49–50 for his full list of those who have made such charges.

[4] See, e.g. H.L.A. Hart, "Positivism and the Separation of Law and Morals" (1958) 71 *Harvard Law Review* 593; H.L.A. Hart, *The Concept of Law*, 2nd edn., with a postscript edited by P.A. Bulloch and J. Raz (Oxford, Clarendon Press, 1994), 207–12.

[5] NB The social thesis assumes different forms in the work of various legal positivists. Compare, for example, the version of it found in Razian "exclusive" positivism (in, for example, J. Raz, *The Authority of Law* (Oxford, Clarendon

thesis, the identification of the law ultimately rests on social facts rather than moral argumentation, the certification of something as law has no moral import and is a morally neutral social fact.[6] This in turn results in the legal positivist project of, "distinguishing the conditions for legality from the conditions for morality,"[7] having the beneficial consequence of promoting clarity and facilitating subjecting the law to critical moral scrutiny, because by holding ascriptions of moral value and legal status apart in the way which it does, legal positivism allows us to see clearly what the law is, before any consideration of its merit or demerit is undertaken.

Schauer's argument seems to proceed, then, from the thought that if we are going to examine something critically, then it is beneficial to have a clear view of its nature in order that the examination can be directed at a target which we have properly in focus. He claims that it is advantageous to identify the law in a way which does not imbue it with presumptive moral merit, and which allows us to suspend our moral judgement until we have a clear view of that which is to be judged.[8] Accordingly, the important task of subjecting the law on some matter to critical moral scrutiny is one which is aided by our first of all identifying it without having our moral faculties engaged. As this view of how law is to be identified is a central part of legal pos-

Press, 1979), ch. 3), with that espoused by a "soft" or "inclusive" positivist or incorporationist (see e.g. Hart, *The Concept of Law*, 2nd edn. (n. 4 *supra*), 250–4; W. Waluchow, *Inclusive Legal Positivism* (Oxford, Clarendon Press, 1994); J. Coleman, "Negative and Positive Positivism" (1982) 11 *Journal of Legal Studies* 139).

[6] Schauer, "Positivism as Pariah" (n. 2 *supra*), 37. The interested reader might want to compare this stance with Joseph Raz's view that: "The claim that what is law and what is not is purely a matter of social fact still leaves it an open question whether or not those social facts by which we identify the law or determine its existence do or do not endow it with moral merit. If they do, it has of necessity a moral character" (Raz, *The Authority of Law* (n. 5 *supra*), 38–9. See also J. Raz, *Practical Reason and Norms*, 2nd edn. (Princeton, NJ, Princeton University Press, 1990) 165–70 in this regard.

[7] Schauer, "Positivism as Pariah" (n. 2 *supra*), 38.

[8] Schauer, "Positivism as Pariah" (n. 2 *supra*), 42.

itivist thinking, this approach to understanding law can draw support from the argument which Schauer makes in the social thesis' name.

Schauer's argument about the beneficial consequences of the social thesis thus has a important bearing upon the question of the criteria which we may use in order to evaluate the success of theories of law. According to Schauer, it is a desirable feature of a legal theory that it subscribes to the social thesis because this latter has the beneficial consequence of promoting clarity and facilitating the moral scrutiny of the law. The ability to promote clearer and more critical thinking about legality, morality, and the relations between them is thus, for Schauer, one of the criteria according to which we may account a legal theory as more or less successful than its rivals. In this sense, then, Schauer subscribes to the beneficial moral consequences thesis: he believes that the beneficial moral consequence of promoting clearer and more critical thinking about the law can constitute grounds for adhering to legal positivism, or, to put it another way, can legitimately feature amongst the criteria in virtue of which we account a legal theory as successful.

In arguing in favour of the social thesis on the ground that it promotes clearer and more critical thinking about the law, Schauer echoes a familiar argument which has been made on legal positivism's behalf several times in the course of recent jurisprudential history.[9] However, to make such an argument in

[9] A version of this argument is sometimes attributed to or made on behalf of H.L.A. Hart, usually based on a certain reading of Hart, *The Concept of Law*, 2nd edn. (n. 4 *supra*), ch. 9, section 3 and H.L.A. Hart, "Positivism and the Separation of Law and Morals" (1958) 71 *Harvard Law Review* 593, section IV. The existence of such attributions to Hart, and to legal positivism in general is noted by, e.g. D. Lyons, "Moral Aspects of Legal Theory", in Marshall Cohen (ed.), *Ronald Dworkin and Contemporary Jurisprudence* (London, Duckworth, 1984); P. Soper, "Choosing a Legal Theory on Moral Grounds", in J. Coleman and E.F. Paul (eds), *Philosophy and Law* (Oxford, Basil Blackwell, 1987); M. Moore, "Law as a Functional Kind" in R.P. George (ed.), *Natural Law Theory: Contemporary Essays* (Oxford, Clarendon Press, 1992); R. Dworkin, "A Reply By Ronald Dworkin" in M. Cohen (ed.), *Ronald Dworkin and Contemporary Jurisprudence*; S. Guest, "Two Strands in Hart's Theory of Law:

legal positivism's name may be to offer it somewhat of a poisoned chalice, for the reason that Schauer's point in favour of the social thesis appears to beg the very question which it seeks to answer, and to emerge as the conclusion of an argument which runs in the wrong direction.

The difficulty arises because Schauer seems to argue in favour of espousing the social thesis on the grounds that so doing will result in the beneficial moral consequence of promoting clearer and more critical thinking about the law. However, the problem with this is that espousing the social thesis will only promote the kind of clearer thinking about the law which could assist in subjecting it to critical moral scrutiny *if* the social thesis is the *correct* way to go about understanding the way in which law is to be identified. The beneficial consequences which Schauer describes, then, will only follow if it is true that law is to be identified in the way the social thesis claims. If alternatively, for example, Ronald Dworkin is correct in his view that law is to be identified by engaging in a process of "constructive interpretation",[10] which aims to show the legal materials at hand in their best moral and political light, then subscribing to the social thesis will certainly not promote the clarity of thought which could aid subjecting the law to critical moral scrutiny, for in so doing, we will not be understanding law correctly.

In other words, the alleged promotion of clearer thinking about the law which results in an increased ability to subject it

A Comment on the *Postscript* to Hart's *The Concept of Law*" in S. Guest (ed.), *Positivism Today* (Aldershot, Dartmouth Publishing Co. Ltd, 1996); N. MacCormick, "A Moralistic Case for A-Moralistic Law" (1985), 20 *Valparaiso Law Review* 1 at 7–11, and L. Murphy, "The Political Question of the Concept of Law" in J.L. Coleman (ed.), *The Postscript: Essays on the Postscript to the Concept of Law* (Oxford, Oxford University Press, forthcoming 2001). The first three authors listed make points similar to those which I go on to make above regarding the problems implicit in attributing this sort of beneficial moral consequences argument to legal positivism; the remaining four are advocates of such an argument in some form.

[10] See R. Dworkin, *Law's Empire* (London, Fontana Press, 1986), chs 2 and 3, and the discussion of Dworkin's work in section B of this chapter, and in Chapter 6.

to moral scrutiny is a consequence which ensues *if* the social thesis is true, and, as such, cannot itself be used to provide argumentative support for its truth. As it stands, Schauer's argument runs in the wrong direction, *from* premises consisting of a claim about the beneficial consequences of espousing a certain theoretical understanding of law, *to* the conclusion that this way of understanding the law is therefore correct.[11] As was explained at the outset of this work,[12] I regard the task of analytical jurisprudence as being that of attempting to identify and explain the nature of law. It is the character of an actually existing social institution which we are after, and it is a basic assumption of this approach that the social institution of law has a particular character which legal theory is attempting to identify and explain. As was discussed in Chapter 1, such an approach presupposes merely this: given that we regard there as being something special about certain forms of social organisation which we account as legal, and given that we recognise that, throughout history, some forms of social organisation have amounted to legal systems and some have not, the only way in which we can begin to investigate what this particular form of social organisation is like, and how it differs from other types of social organisation, is by attempting to isolate and explain those features which are constitutive of it, and which make it into what it is. This is a baseline assumption which all legal theorists in the tradition under consideration here must share, for what else are we doing in legal theory, if not attempting to characterise that which is distinctive about a very powerful and pervasive kind of social institution which does much to shape us and our social world? In light of all this, the peculiar character of Schauer's argument should be readily apparent, for it seems to amount to claiming that, as it would result in beneficial moral consequences if the

[11] On arguments running in the wrong direction, see also Raz, *The Authority of Law* (n. 5 *supra*), 41–2; Raz, "Postema on Law's Autonomy and Public Practical Reasons: A Critical Comment" (1998) 4 *Legal Theory* 1, at 9–11; J. Dickson, "Legal Positivism and Moral Scepticism: An Unholy Alliance?" (Review Article) (1999) 28 *Anglo-American Law Review* 243, at 254–8.

[12] See Chapter 1, section C.

law had certain properties, therefore it does have those properties.

Such a move seems to reduce legal theory to no more than an exercise in wishful thinking: we can choose whether we think of law as having property X or property Y, depending on the beneficial moral consequences which we believe will ensue as a result of this. Schauer explicitly assents to the point about the characterisation of law which we adopt being a matter of choice in the following passage:

> "Thus the moral question is not one about the morality of a definition *per se*, but rather about the moral consequences of a society having this rather than that understanding of some social phenomena . . . Implicit in the foregoing paragraphs is the proposition that the definition of law is a matter of choice rather than discovery, and that moral factors loom large in making that choice".[13]

If, however, we are free to choose whether law has a given property on the basis that it would have better consequences for us if it did, then we are no longer talking about the nature of law, but about something like the nature of ideal law. While this may be a valuable project for novelists and utopian schemers, it is not the enterprise upon which theorists in the analytical jurisprudential tradition are engaged. A commitment to the basic point that law has a certain character which it is the job of legal theory to capture accurately and explain adequately is inherent in the work of all three of the legal theorists—John Finnis, Joseph Raz and Ronald Dworkin—who can be considered as the main protagonists of the present work. Theorists like Finnis and, as I shall explain further shortly, Ronald Dworkin, who believe that it is not possible for a jurisprudential theory to provide an adequate account of law without entering into moral evaluations of it, do so out of a belief that there is something about the character of law as a real social phenomenon which demands that it be understood in this way if it is to be understood adequately. In believing this, and in further believing that law, properly understood, is a morally justified phenomenon, Finnis and

[13] Schauer, "Positivism as Pariah" (n. 2 *supra*), 34.

Dworkin presuppose that law has a particular distinctive character which they are attempting to elucidate. While Finnis and Dworkin differ from Raz in that the criteria of success of their legal theories are to a large extent moral criteria, they share with him the view that there are criteria of success for legal theories, and that those criteria are only met when we characterise law accurately and adequately.[14]

It should also be noted that the points just raised are compatible with the possibility countenanced in Chapter 1 that law may not possess any essential properties. If this is the case, then that it does not possess any such properties will be the correct answer to the question of what law is like. This will not leave much more for analytical jurisprudence to do (except, perhaps, to explain why law does not possess any essential properties?), and will leave the field clear for those approaches to legal theory which attempt to explain various contingent properties which law possesses as a result of the fact that it exists in the context of particular societal conditions prevailing at a particular time and place. In this case, however, it will still not be open to any part of legal theory to choose whether to see law as possessing property X or property Y on the basis that so doing will allegedly result in beneficial moral consequences.

There is much more which could be said regarding Schauer's views on jurisprudential methodology if an examination of those

---

[14] As was indicated in n. 9 *supra*, some commentators have considered whether H.L.A. Hart is also guilty of the charge which I level at Schauer in this chapter. David Lyons raises exactly this point, but then exonerates Hart from any such charge (see Lyons, "Moral Aspects of Legal Theory", in Cohen (ed.), *Ronald Dworkin and Contemporary Jurisprudence* (n. 9 *supra*), 64), while Ronald Dworkin, Stephen Guest and Liam Murphy attribute some kind of beneficial moral consequences argument to Hart, but do not regard it as problematic in the way highlighted above (see Dworkin, "A Reply By Ronald Dworkin", in Cohen (ed.), *Ronald Dworkin and Contemporary Jurisprudence* (n. 9 *supra*), 254–5; Guest, "Two Strands in Hart's Theory of Law: A Comment on the *Postscript* to Hart's *The Concept of Law*" in S. Guest (ed.) *Positivism Today* (n. 9 *supra*); Murphy, "The Political Question of the Concept of Law" in Coleman (ed.), *The Postscript: Essays on the Postscript to the Concept of Law* (n. 9 *supra*)). It is my view that Hart can be cleared of the charge which I have levelled at Schauer, but I cannot discuss this here (see also Chapter 2, n. 9).

views were my main purpose here. For example, Schauer does not appear to be claiming that the ability to engender beneficial moral consequences should be the sole criterion used in judging whether we should espouse legal positivism. He also, very briefly, claims that this approach should be adopted on the grounds that it, "is descriptively accurate as well", at least in the "existing sociological landscape".[15] Unfortunately, the nature of this criterion of descriptive accuracy, and its relation to his argument from beneficial moral consequences are not adequately explained in the article: are these criteria cumulative, or in the alternative, or what? Can a legal theory be successful if it meets one of them but not the other? In any case, Schauer's brief mention of the criterion of descriptive accuracy does not detract from the point that to espouse a beneficial moral consequences argument in favour of legal positivism in the form in which he does fails to take seriously the enterprise of attempting accurately and adequately to characterise what is distinctive about law as an actually existing social institution. So far as the rest of Schauer's views on methodology go: as the main emphasis of this book lies with illuminating the nature of indirectly evaluative legal theory, the present discussion cannot provide a comprehensive analysis of all of those views,[16] nor of beneficial moral consequences arguments in general. Rather, the discussion attempts to illuminate a serious problem with beneficial moral consequences arguments via an analysis of the way in which one such argument features in Schauer's defence of legal positivism.

To sum up, then: if the social thesis promotes clarity in our thinking about law, morality, and the relations between them, then this is so because the social thesis is a correct characterisation of what law is like, and not because viewing law in this way leads to beneficial moral consequences. Contrary to Schauer's apparent assumption, the fact that a legal theory, *if* true, would

---

[15] Both quotations are from Schauer, "Positivism as Pariah" (n. 2 *supra*), 43.

[16] Schauer also discusses jurisprudential methodology in F. Schauer, "Positivism Through Thick and Thin" in B. Bix (ed.), *Analyzing Law: New Essays in Legal Theory* (Oxford, Clarendon Press, 1998).

have the beneficial consequence of facilitating subjecting the law to critical moral scrutiny, cannot constitute grounds for accounting such a theory as more or less successful than its rivals. Such judgements are made by assessing whether a theory of law *is* true, and whether it deepens our understanding of law as a social institution. A theory of law which fulfils these criteria will promote clarity in our thinking about the law and its relation to morality, but this will be *because* the theory is true and explanatorily adequate; the argument cannot run in the other direction, from the alleged clarity which it could provide, to the truth and explanatory adequacy of the theory.[17]

B. Evaluation and Identification: Dworkin's Stance

In "Positivism as Pariah", in addition to arguing that it is a desirable feature of a legal theory that it allows us to identify "pre-morally" those legal rules and institutions which we may then wish to subject to critical moral scrutiny, Schauer also makes a stronger claim regarding the way in which the law is to be identified:

> "all of those who subscribe to some version of anti-positivism, including but not limited to natural law, have a need for some form of identification of that which is then subject to moral evaluation. And so long as the alleged anti-positivisms engage in the process of pre-moral identification of legal items, then it turns out that they have accepted the primary positivist premises which are not at all about the proper uses of the word 'law', but which are rather about the desirability and necessity of first locating that which we then wish to evaluate".[18]

In the passage quoted above, Schauer makes a claim which is stronger than that discussed in the previous section, because

[17] For a discussion of beneficial moral consequences arguments which takes on board and attempts to rebut the "wishful thinking" objection see Murphy, "The Political Question of the Concept of Law" in Coleman (ed.), *The Postscript: Essays on the Postscript to the Concept of Law* (n. 9 *supra*).

[18] Schauer, "Positivism as Pariah" (n. 2 *supra*), 43.

while his initial thesis concerned the *desirability* of engaging in "pre-moral identification"[19] of the law, this passage goes on to make a further appeal to *necessity* in this regard. Schauer is claiming, then, that all legal theorists, no matter the direction of their theoretical leanings, must inevitably have recourse to some pre-moral manner of identifying the "legal items" which they may then wish to go on to morally evaluate.

While I do not wish to address directly Schauer's argument in favour of this second thesis,[20] I do want to point out that he commits himself to a strong claim in propounding it. Schauer is correct to draw our attention to the fact that this thesis may have a wider constituency than is sometimes thought. For example, he recognises the important point that some forms of natural law theory claim to concur with this—at first glance—distinctively positivistic thesis.[21] However, Schauer does not discuss the position of a major twentieth century jurist whose entire approach to understanding the law is premised upon the repudiation of it. Schauer's necessity thesis is interesting in terms of providing a lead-in to Ronald Dworkin's position, then, because Dworkin holds the diametrically opposite view, i.e. that all theorists must necessarily morally evaluate the law, in order to identify what it is.

Dworkin's interpretive approach to understanding law represents a major development in legal theory. Moreover, and especially important for present purposes, this approach brings with it a novel account of correct jurisprudential methodology which provides much for anyone interested in this topic to engage with. In *Law's Empire*, Dworkin begins to elaborate this new vision of law and legal theory by berating prevailing jurisprudential theo-

---

[19] Schauer, "Positivism as Pariah" (n. 2 *supra*), 43.

[20] Nor do I examine the relation between his desirability and necessity theses here.

[21] On this point, see the discussion of Finnis' views in Chapter 4. In that chapter, I claim that it is doubtful whether Finnis' position really is compatible with legal positivism's social thesis. However, this might be due to features which are peculiar to the particular stance which Finnis adopts, and so may not apply to all natural law theories. Unfortunately, I cannot discuss this here, as it would require extensive analysis of possible natural law positions.

ries for their inadequate accounts of the argumentative nature of legal practice, and of the kinds of disagreements which arise within it.[22] Dworkin's view is that these features of the law can only be adequately explained via a methodological revolution wherein legal theorists become participants in the argumentative fray of legal practice, directly disputing for themselves the central elements of that practice. On this model, legal practice, of which, for Dworkin, legal theory is a part,[23] is held to be an *interpretive* practice[24] wherein questions about what law is— questions which range from the most abstract inquiries about the character of a social institution, to the most concrete concerning whether, for example, A is liable to pay damages to B— are answered by interpreting the legal materials at hand according to a certain schema. The schema in question Dworkin terms "constructive interpretation", and consists of an attempt to show those legal materials in their best light, or make of them the best that they can be, in terms of the form or genre to which they are taken to belong.[25]

This process of constructive interpretation comprises two elements. First of all, the outcome of such interpretation must fit existing legal materials to a certain extent. This is necessary in order to distinguish the interpretation of existing legal materials from the pure invention of outcomes which are then labelled legal.[26] Then, within whatever degree of fit is held to be appropriate on a particular occasion, the interpretive process must seek to present those materials in their best light, according to the genre to which they are taken to belong, or, as Dworkin sometimes expresses it, in terms of the purpose or point which they are taken to serve.[27] According to Dworkin, this purpose is

[22] See Dworkin, *Law's Empire* (n. 10 *supra*), chs 1 and 2.

[23] See Dworkin, *Law's Empire* (n. 10 *supra*), 90. This is explained further shortly.

[24] Dworkin, *Law's Empire* (n. 10 *supra*), 50.

[25] Dworkin, *Law's Empire* (n. 10 *supra*), 52–3, and, more generally, chs 2 and 3.

[26] Dworkin, *Law's Empire* (n. 10 *supra*), 66.

[27] Dworkin, *Law's Empire* (n. 10 *supra*), 52–3 and 58–9. This point about the law's genre being expressed in functional terms is explored further in Chapter

that of constraining the power of government via a policing of the use of governmental collective force. The policing in question is designed to ensure that such force can only be used under certain circumstances, namely: "as licensed or required by individual rights and responsibilities flowing from past political decisions about when collective force is justified".[28]

For Dworkin, anyone attempting to interpret the law in its best light according to this purpose or point—that of the justified use of governmental collective force—must bring the political and moral values of justice, fairness, procedural due process and integrity to bear upon their deliberations about the thrust and meaning of past political decisions in order to see the law as informed by those virtues in such a way as to make it as morally coherent as it can be.[29] The political and moral virtues which Dworkin cites are but articulations of the factors which he believes must feed into an interpretation of the law in order for that law so interpreted to be capable of morally justifying state coercion.[30] This renders the best light thesis a morally best light thesis in the case of the law: for Dworkin, law sets the conditions under which the use of collective force is morally justified.[31]

There are thus three main themes which, for present purposes, should be noted as being distinctive of Dworkin's approach to legal theory. First of all, it is an important feature

6. Trade-offs between fit and presenting in the best light are possible in this regard; see Dworkin, *Law's Empire*, 228–32, and, in fact, as a reading of those pages will confirm, the two dimensions are not so independent as might first appear. This aspect of Dworkin's position has attracted criticism from a variety of corners, see e.g. J. Finnis, "On Reason and Authority in Law's Empire" (1987), 6 *Law and Philosophy* 401; N.E. Simmonds, "Imperial Visions and Mundane Practices" (1987) 46 *Cambridge Law Journal* 465.

[28] Dworkin, *Law's Empire* (n. 10 *supra*), 93.

[29] Dworkin, *Law's Empire* (n. 10 *supra*), 176, and, more generally, Chapter 6.

[30] See *Law's Empire* (n. 10 *supra*), chs 6 and 7.

[31] See e.g. Dworkin, *Law's Empire* (n. 10 *supra*), 53, 67 and 90 for the "best light" formulation of the constructive interpretation thesis. For a more extensive exposition of these aspects of Dworkin's position, the interested reader might also consult A. Marmor, *Interpretation and Legal Theory* (Oxford, Clarendon Press, 1992), ch. 3, as well as *Law's Empire* itself.

of Dworkin's position that legal theorists trying to understand law as a social institution, judges deciding cases, lawyers advising clients, and ordinary citizens attempting to understand their rights and responsibilities in terms of the law are all viewed as being engaged upon the same interpretive enterprise. This means that, for Dworkin, there is no difference in kind between the questions, "what is the law on a particular issue?" and "what is the nature of the social institution of law?". The only difference which does exist between these two questions concerns the level of abstraction at which they are asked and attemptedly answered, and this in turn means that, for Dworkin, a theory of law and a theory of adjudication are one and the same thing:

"So no firm line divides jurisprudence from adjudication or any other aspect of legal practice . . . Jurisprudence is the general part of adjudication, silent prologue to any decision at law".[32]

As commentators have noted, this is one feature of Dworkin's position which marks his break with previous approaches to theorising about law in the analytical jurisprudential tradition which have championed a distinction between the nature of law in the abstract and the way in which it is instantiated in particular legal institutions.[33]

Secondly, it is central to Dworkin's account of law that the activity upon which all of the above legal actors are engaged is that of trying to *interpret* the legal materials at hand according to a certain interpretive schema in order to generate a certain kind of result. The foregrounding and elaboration of interpretive argument, and of understanding law as an interpretive concept, is of course also highly distinctive of the Dworkinian legal theoretical enterprise.

Finally, Dworkin contends that the interpretation in question is one which attempts to show the legal materials at hand in their

[32] Dworkin, *Law's Empire* (n. 10 *supra*). Joseph Raz suggests a possible caveat to the identification of Dworkin's theory of law with his theory of adjudication in J. Raz, "The Relevance of Coherence" in J. Raz, *Ethics in the Public Domain* (Oxford, Clarendon Press, 1994), 323.

[33] See, for example, Marmor, *Interpretation and Legal Theory* (n. 31 *supra*), 35.

morally best light. As this task applies as much to legal theorists as it does to, for example, judges, this means that the criteria of success of a legal theory are essentially moral criteria; we succeed as legal theorists when we show the law of our jurisdiction to be as morally coherent and just as possible.

To return to the issue with which this section opened: Schauer claims that it is necessary for all legal theorists first of all to identify without recourse to moral evaluation the legal items or laws which they may then wish to go on to morally evaluate. This is directly challenged by Dworkin because he maintains that we simply cannot know what law is, either as regards individual propositions of law, or at the level of a more abstract account of it as a social institution, until we have engaged for ourselves in the process of constructive interpretation with regard to it. In order to do this, the legal theorist, as much as any other legal actor, must present law in its best light according to the genre to which it is taken to belong. As that genre is the moral justification of the use of governmental collective force, the Dworkinian position stands diametrically opposed to Schauer's: Dworkin claims that we *must* engage in moral evaluation (and justification) of the law in order to know what it is.

C. Dworkin and the Beneficial Moral Consequences Thesis

Having introduced Dworkin's position, I now want to consider the way in which his stance regarding the role of evaluation in identifying the law relates to some of the issues surrounding the beneficial moral consequences thesis which were discussed in section A of this chapter. As was noted in that section, there are some serious difficulties with the beneficial moral consequences argument which Schauer employs in "Positivism as Pariah". If Schauer is correct in his view that we can choose between legal theories for the reasons that he advocates, then jurisprudence appears to be turned into an exercise in wishful thinking, leaving us describing not the nature of law as it is, but rather the nature of law as we would ideally like it to be in order to generate beneficial moral results. In making the argument which he does in legal positivism's name, Schauer does not of course take himself or legal positivism to be describing an ideal form of law, as opposed to law as an actually existing social institution. For all this, however, he does appear to employ the dubious argumentative strategy of arguing from premises about the beneficial moral consequences of law having a certain feature, to the conclusion that therefore law should be understood as having that feature. This does involve arguing from the ideal to the actual in a way which is unacceptable if we hold that it is the job of analytical jurisprudence to attempt to explain accurately and adequately the essential properties of an actually existing social institution.

The question which I now want to address is whether Dworkin is guilty of an analogous form of wishful thinking in holding that one should identify the law by interpreting the legal materials at hand in order to show them in their best moral and political light. At first sight, this distinctive take on the means by which law is to be identified might seem to bring Dworkin close to allowing the ideal to determine the actual in an unacceptable manner. For Dworkin, it seems that there is no "way the law is" (conceived of at whatever level of abstraction) for a legal theorist accurately and adequately to capture, independently of an attempt by that theorist to interpret the law constructively such as to put it in its best moral and political light.

Despite appearances, however, I believe that Dworkin can be acquitted of the "wishful thinking" charge which I level at Schauer. The reason for this is that the way in which the best light thesis feeds into an identification of the law in Dworkin's position is as a general methodological principle which is driven by his view of the character of law as an actually existing social practice, and by his stance on the way in which the kind of social practice which law is should be theoretically understood.

As was discussed in the previous section, it is Dworkin's view that legal practice, of which legal theory is a part, is an interpretive practice, wherein both the character of law as a social institution in an abstract sense, and the content of more concrete propositions of law on some matter, are identified by interpreting the legal materials at hand according to a certain interpretive schema. In my brief characterisation of his position, I mentioned that one main reason why Dworkin advocates this interpretive view of law is because he believes that it provides a better account of the argumentative nature of legal practice, and of disagreements within it, than is provided by rival legal theories. This, however, is to overlook a vital step in his argument, namely that this is the case because, for Dworkin, the interpretive stance which he adopts represents the embodiment of a methodological principle concerning the best way to understand the kind of social practice of which law is an example.

In the part of *Law's Empire* dealing with interpretive concepts in general, Dworkin makes a number of claims regarding the way in which certain social practices must be approached in order for us to gain an adequate understanding of their most significant features.[34] Participants in certain sorts of social practices develop what Dworkin terms a "complex 'interpretive' attitude"[35] towards the rules of those practices. Such an attitude is characterised by two components: "the assumption that the practice does not just exist but has value . . . in short that it has some point", and the realisation on the part of the participants in it that the rules which make up that practice, "are not necessarily what they have always been taken to be, but are instead sensitive to its point".[36] According to Dworkin, when this attitude takes hold amongst the participants in a given social practice, that practice becomes the kind of thing that can only be adequately understood in a certain way, namely by a theorist joining the practice and interpreting for himself what it requires. This means that anyone seeking to understand such a practice must make judgements about what the practice requires, from its most abstract to its most concrete features, which do not

[34] See Dworkin, *Law's Empire* (n. 10 *supra*), ch. 2.

[35] Dworkin, *Law's Empire* (n. 10 *supra*), 47.

[36] Both quotations are from *Law's Empire* (n. 10 *supra*), 47.

merely report upon, but which rival and are competitive with those of the participants in it.

This amounts to a claim that in the case of certain practices, because the practice is of a certain nature, an adequate theoretical understanding of it must mirror the nature of the practice. According to Dworkin, law is one such practice. The interpretive understanding of law thus delivers a more adequate account of the argumentative character of that practice, because argumentative practices such as law in which the nature and point of the practice is a controversial matter so far as participants in it are concerned, can only be understood properly if the theorist himself joins in the argument and offers a rival interpretation of that practice.[37]

With this in mind, let us recall the worry with which this section began, i.e. that Dworkin's distinctive take on the means by which law is to be identified appears to bring him close to arguing from an ideal of how law morally ought to be, to the conclusion that therefore this is how law is to be understood, in a manner analogous to Schauer's problematic use of a beneficial moral consequences argument. My tentative acquittal of Dworkin from this "wishful thinking" charge should by now have been fleshed out a little. Dworkin does not smuggle in an illegitimate form of argument in contending that an interpretation which shows the law in its best moral light is to be the guiding principle in determining what the law is, because the constructive interpretation thesis is but one aspect of a general methodological principle which informs all of his thinking about the law, and which is driven by his view of the character of law as an actually existing social practice of a certain kind. For Dworkin, law *is* an interpretive practice which must be identified and understood in a certain way, namely via the process of constructive interpretation. This is not because of wishful thinking that it would be morally better if the law were that way/because of the alleged beneficial moral consequences of

[37] For a critical discussion of this aspect of Dworkin's position, and of the various means by which he attempts to support it, see Marmor, *Interpretation and Legal Theory* (n. 31 *supra*), 40–60.

101

thinking of it that way, but rather because of the way that law as an actually existing phenomenon is anyway—namely that it is an argumentative social practice with a point, wherein that which the practice requires is sensitive to that point. According to Dworkin, the actually existing character of law as an interpretive practice of this kind dictates that it must be understood in a certain way if it is to be understood adequately, namely by legal theorists constructively interpreting that practice in order to show it in its best light according to the genre to which it is taken to belong.

Unlike Schauer's beneficial moral consequences thesis, then, Dworkin's argument proceeds in the right direction: *from* a claim about the character of the social practice of law, via a contention that practices of that sort require to be understood in a certain way, *to* the constructive interpretation thesis which then imports the notion of seeing law in its best light in order to determine what it is. Dworkin's contention is that law *is* an interpretive practice; that is just what law is like, and this is why we have to identify and understand it via constructive interpretation. His argument is not that, as beneficial moral consequences would ensue from seeing law in its morally best light, therefore law is that which we identify via the process of constructive interpretation. For Dworkin, it is not that an account of how it would be best for law to be, morally speaking, is illegitimately used in order to argue in support of how law actually is, but rather that constructively interpreting the law according to a schema which makes reference to how it morally ought to be is the only way to identify and provide an adequate explanation of law as it actually is.

Dworkin's position, therefore, does not turn legal theory into an exercise in wishful thinking in the way which Schauer's beneficial moral consequences argument in favour of legal positivism implicitly does. Dworkin is concerned with characterising law as it is, not as we would like it to be in order to engender the best possible moral results.

6

What's the Point of Law? Dworkinian Methodology and the Argument from Law's Function

In this chapter I return to the main topic of the present work, namely the nature of indirectly evaluative legal theory. Ronald Dworkin's work presents a strong challenge to this methodological approach, in that Dworkin claims that it is necessary for a legal theorist to engage in moral and political argument in order to understand law properly. A major strand in his thinking in this regard is the idea that all legal theories adequate to their task must develop and defend a political theory about the point or function of law in the course of providing an account of it. It is the task of this chapter to examine the role which arguments about law's function play in Dworkin's vision of correct jurisprudential methodology, and to challenge his claim that all adequate legal theories must have recourse to arguments about the function of law, at least in the sense in which he intends this claim.

A. Constructive Interpretation and the Function of Law

In order to begin examining the role which arguments about law's function play in Dworkin's view of jurisprudential methodology, it is necessary to consider where he stands as regards the moral evaluation and moral justification theses, and why.[1] We

---

[1] To recap.: the moral evaluation thesis states that it is necessary to morally evaluate the law in order to understand it adequately; the moral justification

can begin to approach this matter by taking a closer look at the constructive interpretation thesis which, as was discussed in the last chapter, is central to Dworkin's account of law. [2]

In discussing the nature of interpretive concepts in *Law's Empire*,[3] Dworkin tells us that to constructively interpret something is: "a matter of imposing purpose on an object or practice so as to make of it the best possible example of the form or genre to which it is taken to belong".[4]

As this formulation indicates, the idea of form or genre plays an important role in the constructive interpretation process. When we constructively interpret an object or practice we aim to show it in its best light, and we succeed in doing that when we make of it the best possible example of the form or genre to which it is taken to belong. The form or genre of an object or practice is thus crucial to the constructive interpretation process for it acts as a constraint upon, and gives meaning to, the idea of showing something in its best light.

As has already been documented in my exposition of his position in Chapter 5, Dworkin regards law as an interpretive concept. What, then, is the form or genre according to which we should attempt to show law in the best possible light? It is my contention that, for Dworkin, the form or genre of law is given in terms of his statement of the abstract point or purpose which he regards that social institution as serving. That abstract point or purpose is given as follows:

"Our discussions about law by and large assume, I suggest, that the most abstract and fundamental point of legal practice is to constrain the power of government in the following way. Law insists that force not be used or withheld, no matter how useful that would be to ends in view, no matter how beneficial or noble these ends, except as licensed or required by individual rights and responsibil-

---

thesis states that it is necessary to hold the law to be morally justified in order to understand it adequately.

[2] See Chapter 5, section B.

[3] See R. Dworkin, *Law's Empire* (London, Fontana Press, 1986), ch. 2.

[4] Dworkin, *Law's Empire* (n. 3 *supra*), 52.

ities flowing from past political decisions about when collective force is justified".[5]

As this passage should make clear, according to Dworkin, the point or function of law, abstractly conceived, is to police and justify the use of governmental collective force. Dworkin claims that this statement of the point of law is intended to provide us with "an account that organizes further argument about law's character".[6] As is implicit in this claim, and as is discussed further below, this postulated point or function of law operates so as to provide the constraints which are necessary in order for the constructive interpretation process to get underway. In constructively interpreting the law, we should try to show it in the best possible light in terms of the abstract point or function which Dworkin ascribes to it—that of justifying the use of collective force—and this is exactly what Dworkin attempts to do in the remainder of *Law's Empire* in developing his account of law as integrity.[7] This being the case, I regard this abstract point or function of law as demarcating the form or genre to which Dworkin takes law to belong. Dworkin thus characterises the kind of thing which law is taken to be and which organises further debate about its character in functional terms: in constructively interpreting the law, we aim to put it in its best light as that which justifies the use of collective force.

In terms of the terminology introduced in Chapter 3, then, it follows that Dworkin's theory of law is a directly evaluative theory, i.e. one which contains or entails one or more directly evaluative propositions concerning features of the law.[8] This is so because, for Dworkin, in order to identify and understand the law we must interpret it so as to show it in its best light in terms of the form or genre to which it is taken to belong. That form or genre—the kind of thing which law is taken to be and which organises further debate about its character—is the justified use

[5] Dworkin, *Law's Empire* (n. 3 *supra*), 93.

[6] Dworkin, *Law's Empire* (n. 3 *supra*), 93.

[7] On law as integrity, see Dworkin, *Law's Empire* (n. 3 *supra*), chs 6 and 7.

[8] See Chapter 3, section C.

of collective force. Combined with Dworkin's point that those involved in both jurisprudence and adjudication must engage in the same process of constructive interpretation in order to know what law is,[9] this means that legal theorists, as much as any other legal actors, must themselves attempt to see law in its best moral and political light, and attempt to evaluate the conditions under which collective force really is justified, in order to identify and understand the law. This clearly involves the legal theorist in making directly evaluative judgements about features of the law in order to identify and explain law's character. To recap on the discussion in Chapter 3: directly evaluative judgements differ in kind from indirectly evaluative judgements in that the latter pick out features of the law as important or significant to explain, rather than as good or justified, as is the case with the former type of judgements.[10]

This being so, Dworkin's position on the moral evaluation and moral justification theses is—at least in respect of the conclusions which he draws—the same as Finnis'. For Dworkin, it is necessary for a legal theory to morally or directly evaluate the law in order to understand it and, moreover, as the passage quoted above concerning Dworkin's view of the point or function of law makes clear,[11] it is also the case for Dworkin that a successful jurisprudential theory will hold the law to be a morally justified phenomenon. Law, for Dworkin, is nothing other than the justified use of collective force. According to his account, we do not have a proper grasp of what law is until we have asked what would justify collective force in a given jurisdiction, and until we have constructively interpreted the legal practices of that jurisdiction so as to see them in their best light as practices which properly police and constrain governmental coercion.[12]

---

[9] See the exposition of Dworkin's views given in Chapter 5, section B.

[10] The points raised at the end of section A of Chapter 3 concerning equating moral and direct evaluation also hold for this chapter and for the one which follows.

[11] See p. 104 *supra*.

[12] It should be noted that Dworkin's view of what it is for the law to be morally justified is different from Finnis'. For Finnis, the law is morally justified

In Dworkin's position, both the moral evaluation and moral justification theses are driven by his view of the function of law. As should be clear from the foregoing, once Dworkin's view of law's point or function has been accepted, then we have already embraced the idea that law is a morally justified phenomenon which demands moral evaluation on the part of a legal theorist attempting to understand it. This being so, it should be evident that Dworkin's idea of law's function has far-reaching ramifications as regards which methodological stance a theory of law should adopt. However, one would not necessarily suspect that this is the case from the way in which Dworkin introduces this thesis in *Law's Empire*, where he seems keen to play down its significance and possible ramifications, presenting it merely as a starting point which is necessary in order to get us all into the same interpretive ballpark.

As is pointed out several times in *Law's Empire*, we cannot have meaningful debate or disagreement about something unless we are all, to some extent, talking about the same thing.[13] This being so, Dworkin claims that the genre or abstract point of law which he postulates is merely a suggestion put forward in order to get us all into the same preliminary ballpark as regards further debates about law's character.[14] Other caveats and qualifications follow, with Dworkin stating repeatedly that he is merely providing a provisional structure within which discussion and disagreement about law can take place, and further describing the characterisation of law's function which he settles on as "suitably airy" and "sufficiently abstract and uncontroversial".[15] In the remainder of this chapter, I claim that Dworkin's view of

in that it is directed towards resolving the co-ordination problems of a community for the common good of that community, a state of affairs which results in its generating a general moral obligation to obey it. For Dworkin, that the law is morally justified means that law is viewed as that which constrains the use of governmental collective force according to the proper justificatory schema and so upholds individual rights and responsibilities.

[13] See e.g. Dworkin, *Law's Empire* (n. 3 *supra*), 43–4, 90–2.

[14] Dworkin, *Law's Empire* (n. 3 *supra*), 93.

[15] Again, see Dworkin, *Law's Empire* (n. 3 *supra*), 93.

law's point or function is very far from the provisional, uncontroversial and sufficiently abstract organising idea which he presents it as. The general thrust of my argument is that the view of law's function which Dworkin advocates defines in a fairly concrete sense the limits of and possibilities for a theoretical understanding of the law, and that it does so in a way which closes down many of the most important questions which can be asked within jurisprudence before they can be properly raised. In short, Dworkin's view of law's function does not just get us all into the same interpretive ballpark, but rather defines the composition, strategy and stance of one particular jurisprudential team.

We can begin by considering Dworkin's claims that his conception of law's genre or function is "sufficiently abstract" and "suitably airy".[16] The sufficiently abstract point is important because it allows Dworkin to claim that his view of law's function does not cut down too severely the options which are open to us in interpreting the law. This, in turn, is important because Dworkin's whole approach is concerned with explaining the nature of argument and disagreement within the law, and, in keeping with this aim, he must avoid closing down the possibility of such disagreement by imposing a fixed view of what law is from the outset.

There is, however, a problem with all of this, because while the "sufficiently abstract" point might work as regards a judge interpreting a particular, more concrete legal issue in light of the abstract genre constraints which Dworkin postulates, it runs into difficulties when the interpretation under consideration is that which Dworkin alleges is offered by legal theorists, i.e. an interpretation at the most abstract level of the character of law as a social institution. The reason for this is that, in the case of legal theory, the point or genre which Dworkin postulates does not so much provisionally designate in an abstract fashion the arena within which more concrete competing interpretations of law may vie, but rather itself pins down some centrally important

---

[16] Dworkin, *Law's Empire* (n. 3 *supra*), 93.

aspects of law's character. Unlike judges, legal theorists are not using the abstract constraints provided by some postulated view of law's function in order to interpret a more concrete set of legal materials in light of those constraints. Rather, legal theorists are attempting to answer the question of what the law, abstractly conceived, is like, a question which—for Dworkin at least—demands an answer which includes reference to law's overall point or function. However, Dworkin's own stipulation of the genre or point of law at the outset of the inquiry already answers this question to a very significant extent. The constructive interpretation thesis thus appears to run into difficulties when considered as a means of answering those most abstract questions with which legal theory is concerned.

To explain further: Dworkin contends that constructively interpreting the law is the way to proceed as regards the questions of legal theorists and practitioners of law alike.[17] One of the questions which legal theorists might want to take a view on, and, according to Dworkin, which they must take a view on,[18] is whether law has a point or function, and, if it does, what that function might be. However, it does not seem to make sense to talk of legal theorists undertaking the constructive interpretation process in order to ascertain, for example, which view of law's genre or function displays it in its best light according to the form or genre to which law is taken to belong, because at this abstract level of interpretation, that which is supposed to act as a constraint on such interpretations, and to designate the arena within which they must vie—namely the idea of law's genre or abstract function—is itself one of the main issues to be addressed by legal theory.

The problem which I am trying to elucidate arises because, as was discussed in Chapter 5, Dworkin wants the constructive interpretation thesis to apply both as regards the determination of concrete propositions of law, and in respect of an abstract account of the character of law as a social institution. In order

[17] See, once again, Dworkin, *Law's Empire* (n. 3 *supra*), 90, and the discussion in Chapter 5, section B.

[18] This is discussed further as the chapter proceeds.

to provide the requisite constraints on more concrete interpretations of what the law on a particular issue is, some abstract view of law's function or genre must remain fixed in place. However, when we then want to undertake the same interpretive process in the service of identifying and understanding that abstract view of law's genre or function itself, a problem arises because that which is, so to speak, up for interpretive grabs, is also that which is supposed to be providing a constraint on the interpretive process. This leaves Dworkin with two choices. He can hold law's genre or function to be fixed, in order to lend the necessary constraints to more concrete interpretations of the law on particular issues, but if he does so, then he appears to be stipulating, and exempting from the constructive interpretation process this abstract notion of law's function itself. Alternatively, he can allow that law's most abstract point or genre, too, is up for interpretive grabs, in which case he is left with the question of what is supposed to provide the constraints on interpretation or designate the arena within which competing interpretations may vie at this level. It is my view that Dworkin does not address this latter question very extensively because in *Law's Empire* he is concerned in the first instance with demonstrating how the constructive interpretation thesis provides an account of the means by which more concrete legal questions are to be decided, rather than with how it fares in terms of answering the abstract questions of legal theory. This is not to say, of course, that Dworkin is not concerned with the questions of legal theory, but rather merely to point out that his answers to those questions are to be found by abstracting from the more concrete constructive interpretation process which applies in respect of judges deciding cases, and which is the primary driving force of the discussions in *Law's Empire*. In other words, I regard Dworkin's theory of law as developing out of and being driven by his account of adjudication, rather than *vice versa*. This being the case, in order to give an account of judicial decision-making as he understands it, Dworkin does require to hold law's genre constant in order to generate constraints upon the constructive interpretation process undertaken by judges. I wish to claim that this is exactly

110

what his position does: stipulates at the outset and holds constant a particular substantive view of law's genre or function in order to allow for the interpretation of more concrete legal issues in light of it, whilst simultaneously claiming that this does not close down debate on the question of the character of law, abstractly conceived, because the view of law's function which is introduced is uncontroversial, provisional, and sufficiently abstract in nature.

Moreover, as a result of fixing law's function in the way in which he does, allegedly as a preliminary step merely to get us all into the same interpretive ballpark, Dworkin also fixes to a large extent the character of law so far as the abstract questions of legal theory are concerned. Once he has got the genre or function point in place, many of the questions which legal theorists should want to ask, concerning, for example, whether law has an overall point or function at all, and whether that point means that law, properly understood, is a morally meritorious or morally justified phenomenon, have already been answered. The benefit of the relative abstractness which Dworkin requires in order that his view of law's genre or function operates merely so as to get us all into the same ballpark, thus organising and making possible further debate on more concrete legal issues, is lost when the interpretive process moves to those abstract climes which the legal theorist inhabits.

The other main points which Dworkin makes in support of his notion of law's function are that it is relatively uncontroversial in nature, and that it is put forward merely as a provisional suggestion.[19] If this truly were the case, then Dworkin would have ways of responding to the charge just made that, as regards the more abstract end of the interpretive spectrum, the view of law's function which he propounds quite concretely fixes the answers to certain important questions about law's character, rather than being a sufficiently abstract organising principle which merely marks out the arena for further debate about those questions. Dworkin could then claim either that this does not matter, as these are answers

---

[19] Dworkin, *Law's Empire* (n. 3 *supra*), 93.

upon which all are agreed, and are thus not important or live issues in jurisprudential debate, or, alternatively, that he is willing to engage seriously with and possibly be persuaded by potential challenges to his view of law's genre or function. It is doubtful, however, that Dworkin can successfully claim that the view of law's genre or function which he advocates is either uncontroversial or provisional in nature. This is best illustrated by considering Dworkin's response when faced with jurisprudential theories which challenge his view of the function of law.

Certain proponents of legal positivism strongly dispute Dworkin's claim that it is an uncontroversial matter amongst legal theorists that law has the abstract point of justifying governmental coercion which *Law's Empire* assigns to it. Positivists such as H.L.A. Hart and Joseph Raz adopt what might be called an "institutional approach", whereby law is characterised not by its overall function or goal but rather by its method: by the way, or the variety of ways, in which it does the things it does in society.[20] On such an approach, the primary focus of jurisprudential inquiry lies with those distinctive legal institutions and processes which reveal the structure and mode of law's operation, and which help us to place and understand legal institutions in relation to other social and political institutions. Many theorists in this tradition do not even accept that law has one overall point or function, let alone that a whole tradition of jurisprudential thought converges upon one view of law's function such as to render it uncontroversial. While such theorists may accept that individual laws, or areas of law can have one or more functions, it is not part of their thinking that law as a social institution has one overall function or purpose.[21]

[20] See e.g. H.L.A. Hart, "Comment" in R. Gavison (ed.), *Issues in Contemporary Legal Philosophy* (Oxford, Clarendon Press, 1987), 37; J. Raz, *The Authority of Law* (Oxford, Clarendon Press, 1979), ch. 6; J. Raz, "The Problem About the Nature of Law" in J. Raz, *Ethics in the Public Domain* (Oxford, Clarendon Press, 1994).

[21] See e.g. H.L.A. Hart, *The Concept of Law*, 2nd edn., with a postscript edited by P.A. Bulloch and J. Raz (Oxford, Clarendon Press, 1994), 248–50; J. Raz, "Postema on Law's Autonomy and Public Practical Reasons: A Critical Comment" (1998) 4 *Legal Theory* 1, especially at 2–4.

How, then, does Dworkin deal with this kind of challenge to his allegedly uncontroversial and provisional view of law's point or function? In the main, he does so by attempting to minimise the existence of such challenges, and, where it is necessary to recognise them, to re-interpret them in terms more akin to his own:

> "No doubt there are exceptions to this claim, theories that challenge rather than elaborate the connection it assumes between law and the justification of coercion. But not as many as there might seem to be at first glance".[22]

This passage ends with a reference to a note in which Dworkin claims that legal positivism must attempt to understand law as having the function of justifying state coercion if it is to be at all plausible as an account of law.[23] Moreover, although with a slightly different spin on it, Dworkin also interprets legal positivism as being committed to a very similar view of how state coercion *is* to be justified as that which is advocated in his own theory; namely a view concerning the adequate protection of individual rights from governmental interference.[24]

Contrary to his official declarations of its provisional nature, then, Dworkin appears to believe that espousing a view regarding law's point or function, and indeed espousing a view very similar to that which he offers in this regard, is essential to any adequate legal theory. His position, in effect, is that there is no alternative to the approach which he adopts: all legal theories which are worth taking seriously presuppose or depend upon arguments about law's function which are broadly similar to those advocated in his own theory: "A conception of law *must* explain how what it takes to be law provides a general justification for the exercise of coercive power by the state".[25]

[22] Dworkin, *Law's Empire* (n. 3 *supra*), 93–4.

[23] Dworkin, *Law's Empire* (n. 3 *supra*), 429–30, n. 3.

[24] See e.g. Dworkin, "A Reply by Ronald Dworkin" in Cohen (ed.), *Ronald Dworkin and Contemporary Jurisprudence* (London, Duckworth, 1984), 248; Dworkin, *Law's Empire* (n. 3 *supra*), ch. 4, and 429–30, n. 3.

[25] Dworkin, *Law's Empire* (n. 3 *supra*), 190 (emphasis added).

In the remainder of the chapter, I examine this claim further via a comparison of Dworkin and Raz's views on the role which arguments about law's function play in their respective legal theories. My aim will be to cast doubt on Dworkin's thesis that any adequate jurisprudential theory must explain how law functions so as to provide a general justification for the exercise of state coercion. In section B below, I proceed by arguing that one major rival to Dworkin's position—namely the account of law offered by Joseph Raz—does not involve viewing law as having the function of providing a justification for state coercion. This is intended to show that Dworkin's view of law's function is not uncontroversial, and also to demonstrate that there is ground for an adequate theory of law to occupy which does not require recourse to morally or directly evaluative arguments in favour of law having a certain function. In section C, I continue my critical analysis of Dworkin's views by discussing some considerations which militate against accepting his particular manner of employing arguments from law's function in supporting the account of law which he offers.

B. Dworkin vs. Raz: The Argument From Law's Function

It is Dworkin's contention, then, that legal positivism, despite protestations to the contrary by some its exponents, must rely upon an appeal to law's function or purpose if it is adequately to defend the account of law which it offers. The particular argument about law's function which Dworkin ascribes to positivism thus interpreted has to do with an issue which loomed large in the last chapter, namely that of the nature of those tests used to identify the law. It is, of course, a central tenet of legal positivism that the identification of legal rules turns upon a social facts test, such that the law may be identified without recourse to moral argument. Dworkin contends that it is in this thesis—often referred to as the social thesis—that legal positivism's argument from law's function can be found:

"The important question is not, however, whether Hart or any other particular legal philosopher is committed to the thesis that the test for law must make law reasonably demonstrable. That thesis is connected to a more general theory of law—in particular to a picture of law's function. This is the theory that law provides a settled, public and dependable set of standards for private and official conduct, standards whose force cannot be called into question by some individual official's perception of policy or morality".[26]

According to this reading, legal positivists view the function of law as being to uphold rule of law ideals, especially "the ideal of protected expectations".[27] This view of law's function can be used in order to bolster the account of law which positivism presents, and, in particular, to provide support for the social thesis as a correct characterisation of an aspect of the law. In maintaining that the law is to be identified via social facts, and without need of recourse to moral argumentation, the social thesis can gain support from the idea that it is the function of law to uphold the ideal of protected expectations by promulgating a clear and dependable set of publicly ascertainable standards upon which individuals can rely in organising their lives.[28]

Joseph Raz has conceded that, in arguing in support of his version of the social thesis—namely the sources thesis[29]—he does indeed appeal to considerations which bear some resemblance to those which Dworkin raises in the above passage. At several points in his work, Raz makes the case for the sources thesis on the grounds that this doctrine accounts for certain aspects of our understanding of the functions which law is

[26] Dworkin, "A Reply by Ronald Dworkin" in Cohen (ed.), *Ronald Dworkin and Contemporary Jurisprudence* (n. 24 *supra*), 248. This passage also appears in R. Dworkin, "A Reply to Critics", in R. Dworkin, *Taking Rights Seriously* (Cambridge, Mass., Harvard University Press, 1977), at 347.

[27] Dworkin, *Law's Empire* (n. 3 *supra*), 117.

[28] In outlining Dworkin's argument, I am ignoring the complications which might ensue if it is to be applied to so called soft or inclusive legal positivism (see Chapter 5, n. 5 for references to works on soft or inclusive positivism). As Raz is not a soft positivist, and as it is his work which I am focusing upon here, these need not detain us in the discussion which follows.

[29] On the sources thesis, see Raz, *The Authority of Law* (n. 20 *supra*), ch. 3.

intended to serve. I wish to survey some of these arguments in the course of the following discussion, in order to contrast them with the type of argument from law's function which Dworkin employs in his own theory, and which he attributes to many other such theories on his reading of them.[30]

In his essay, "Legal Positivism and the Sources of Law",[31] Raz draws our attention to the commonplace that in order for us to live together in society and to have the opportunity to pursue our different goals, certain schemes of co-operation, co-ordination and forbearance are necessary. People have very different views as to how society should be organised, and, Raz claims, it is thus a fundamentally important function of the law that it can pick out from those many differing private views, a public view of what is to be done, and of how we are to act and to refrain from acting which can lay claim to be binding upon all the members of a society regardless of their possible disagreement with it. It should be noted that Raz certainly does not claim that any solution to a society's co-ordination and other problems which the law picks out in this manner should be regarded as truly being morally authoritative or morally binding upon the members of that society. To put the matter in Razian terms, this will depend upon whether the solution which the law picks out meets the conditions specified in the normal justification thesis,[32] and whether, even if it does, there are conflicting

[30] It should be noted that, as my concerns lie not with the substance of Raz's arguments about the nature of law, but rather with the methodological presuppositions underlying them, I neither purport to endorse, nor fully to do justice to those arguments here. Further reading in this regard is signalled in the notes accompanying the text.

[31] In Raz, *The Authority of Law* (n. 20 *supra*), ch. 3. See especially 50–2.

[32] "The normal justification thesis: The normal and primary way to establish that a person should be acknowledged to have authority over another person involves showing that the alleged subject is likely better to comply with reasons which apply to him (other than the alleged authoritative directives) if he accepts the directives of the alleged authority as authoritatively binding, and tries to follow them, than if he tries to follow the reasons which apply to him directly": Raz, "Authority, Law and Morality" in Raz, *Ethics in the Public Domain* (n. 20 *supra*), 214.

reasons which outweigh the normal justification thesis on a particular occasion.[33] Rather, the claim is that, given the co-ordination etc. problems to which societies are inevitably subject, it is an important function of the law that it issues purportedly authoritative rulings which *claim* to be binding upon those to whom they are addressed simply in virtue of the fact that they issue from the authority in question, and regardless of whether they are justified on other grounds, or according to other beliefs which members of the society in question have. According to Raz, it is part of how we understand the kind of thing which law purports to be, and the kind of functions which it is attempting to perform, that we understand it as issuing directives which claim to be authoritative in this manner. The sources thesis gains support from this argument concerning one of the functions of law, because, Raz claims, it will only be possible for law to issue purportedly authoritative rulings which claim to be binding upon those to whom they are addressed simply in virtue of the fact that they issue from the authority in question, if there is a way of identifying those rulings which is publicly ascertainable, and which does not require resort to moral argument.[34]

For all this, however, fundamental differences remain between Raz and Dworkin's respective stances regarding the role which arguments about law's function play in lending support to legal theories. There are two main points of contention between them which I wish to highlight here. First of all, unlike Dworkin, Raz does not hold that law can be characterised in terms of having any one overall function, of whatever nature. Secondly, although Raz does make use of arguments concerning the several functions which law might serve in the course of developing and supporting his account of the nature of law, these are not directly

[33] See e.g. Raz, *The Authority of Law* (n. 20 *supra*), ch. 12; J. Raz, "The Obligation to Obey: Revision and Tradition" and J. Raz, "Authority, Law and Morality" in Raz, *Ethics in the Public Domain* (n. 20 *supra*); J. Raz, *The Morality of Freedom* (Oxford, Clarendon Press, 1986), Pt I.

[34] See Raz, *The Authority of Law* (n. 20 *supra*), 50–2. For a more complex series of arguments in favour of the sources thesis, and based on law's authoritative nature, see Raz, "Authority, Law and Morality" in Raz, *Ethics in the Public Domain* (n. 20 *supra*).

or morally evaluative arguments in favour of law having certain functions.

To begin with the first point: as was already mentioned at the end of the previous section, Raz, like Hart before him, is not in the business of being guided by *any* conception of *the* one overall function of law in his characterisation of this social institution. Providing publicly ascertainable standards of conduct which claim to express an authoritative and binding judgement about how members of society ought to behave is one important function which law performs, but it is just that: one function amongst many others and potential others which this social institution can carry out. Other such functions may include, for example, settling unregulated disputes, providing services and redistributing goods, strengthening national identity and unity, and influencing and changing societal values.[35] Unlike Dworkin, then, Raz does not regard law as having one overall function in terms of which it is to be characterised:

"Justice, I believe, is not the law's ultimate aspiration, for there is no one moral virtue that all law by its nature aspires to, other than to be good: that is to be as it should be. This means that it should be just, and generous, and compassionate and many other things. It is important to remember that the law has no specific function (though it, or parts of it, have many such functions)".[36]

Secondly, it is important to note that Dworkin affirms—whereas Raz strongly denies—that providing support for the sources thesis *via* an argument concerning one of law's functions involves a judgement about the moral value of certain aspects of law or a directly or morally evaluative argument in favour of law having a certain function. To explain: for Dworkin, understanding the law as having a function, and, more specifically, understanding it in terms of the function which he assigns to it, is an attempt to make the best moral sense of what the law is up to. The aim is to show law in its best light accord-

[35] See Raz, *The Authority of Law* (n. 20 *supra*), ch. 9.

[36] Raz, "Postema on Law's Autonomy and Public Practical Reasons: A Critical Comment" (n. 21 *supra*), 1–20, at 2.

ing to its genre—the justified use of governmental force. As this methodological presupposition underlies all of Dworkin's thinking about the law, he believes that legal positivism is also best understood as appealing to an argument about law's function which tries to present law in its best moral light: "The conventionalist conception of law . . . is interpretive . . . It argues that this way of describing legal practice shows that practice in its best light".[37]

This, however, is not the sense in which Razian positivism makes appeal to one of the functions of law in arguing in support of the sources thesis. Raz has attempted to state the difference between his own position, and that of Dworkin, as follows:

> "it is misleading to regard the thesis and argument explained here as moral ones. The argument is indeed evaluative, but in the sense that any good theory of society is based on evaluative considerations in that its success is in highlighting important social structures and processes, and every judgement of importance is evaluative".[38]

This passage, with its implicit reference to two different types of evaluative argument, brings us back to the discussion of indirectly evaluative legal theory in Chapters 2 and 3. The points raised in those chapters were intended to dispel the myth that legal positivists such as Raz seek a "value-free" account of the nature of law, and to explain the way in which such theories require recourse to propositions which I termed indirectly evaluative propositions in order to support the accounts of law which

[37] Dworkin, *Law's Empire* (n. 3 *supra*), 116. "Conventionalism" is the Dworkinian alter-ego of legal positivism, in which this latter is read as an interpretive conception of law (see *Law's Empire*, Chapter 4). Dworkin does not claim that conventionalism is the only possible reading of legal positivism, but his discussion of it does reveal the role which he believes arguments from law's function must play in positivism if it is to be capable of providing a plausible account of law. Moreover, Dworkin also attributed the functional argument outlined above to legal positivism even before his re-interpretation of it along conventionalist lines in *Law's Empire*, as is clear from, Dworkin, "A Reply by Ronald Dworkin" in Cohen (ed.), *Ronald Dworkin and Contemporary Jurisprudence* 248 (n. 24 *supra*) (quoted on p 115 above).

[38] Raz, "Authority, Law and Morality" in Raz, *Ethics in the Public Domain* (n. 20 *supra*), 235 (internal footnote omitted).

they offer. This latter point is vital in the present context, for, as is explained further below, Raz's argument about one of law's functions does involve indirectly evaluative judgements concerning features of the law, but it is not an attempt to ascribe one overall function to law in order to show it in its best moral light.

For Raz, then, to support the sources thesis with an argument about one of law's functions—namely the function of providing publicly ascertainable standards of conduct which purport to express a binding and authoritative judgement regarding how society is to be organised—is merely to claim that the sources thesis reflects and explains one important aspect of the way in which we understand the social institution of law to function. Raz's claim is that the existence of social institutions which purport to issue authoritative directives in the manner and for the reasons described above is an important feature of social life. Such institutions will evidently have a pervasive influence upon our lives in society and upon our practical reasoning processes, because they issue purportedly authoritative and binding directives which, in effect, demand that we lay aside our own views as to how we should behave regarding certain matters, and follow the view which is publicly marked out by the law, on pain of otherwise being subject to its coercive force. Whether or not those legal institutions are justified in so doing, that is the manner in which they invariably operate, and this is an important feature of the law to be explained. In making the case outlined above, that the sources thesis explains how it is possible for law to perform one of its central functions, Raz is thus not trying to show the law in its best moral light. He does not attempt to highlight the moral or immoral substance of what the law is up to on a particular occasion, nor to consider whether institutions issuing purportedly authoritative and binding directives are of moral worth. Rather, the claim is that the existence of such institutions, and the particular way in which they function, is of importance in understanding the law, and in understanding how our social world is shaped by its presence.

Raz is thus supporting his claim that the sources thesis explains how law can perform certain functions with evaluative judgements concerning that which is important about the way in which law operates. However, although this attribution of importance to those aspects of the law which the sources thesis reflects and explains does involve evaluation, this is not a direct or moral evaluation, never mind vindication, of the content or substance of what the law is up to, or of the means by which it operates. Raz seeks to highlight the importance of a social institution which claims to have authority over us, and which hence issues directives which purport to impinge upon our practical reasoning processes in a certain manner. Whether or not the law really does have authority over us, whether or not we ought to accept that the law's directives are binding upon us, and whether or not the existence of such purported authorities are a morally good or bad thing, are not Raz's concern in mounting the argument from law's function in favour of the sources thesis outlined above. In employing the kind of argument in favour of the sources thesis which Raz does, a legal theorist thus need not concern himself with whether the function of providing publicly ascertainable standards of conduct identifiable without recourse to moral argument is of moral merit or demerit. Rather, all that he needs to be able to ascertain is that this is one of the things which law invariably does, that it is a significant aspect of its mode of operation, and that it plays an important role in how those subject to the law think about the functions which it is intended to serve, and use law in the course of reasoning about what they ought to do.

The distinction implicit in the foregoing paragraphs between evaluation which picks out certain features of the law as central to our social experience and hence important to explain on the one hand, and evaluation which returns a moral judgement on the goodness or otherwise of those features of the law on the other is, of course, none other than the distinction between indirect evaluation and direct evaluation which I discussed in Chapter 3. The argument from one of law's functions outlined above thus demonstrates the sense in which Raz requires to have recourse to indirect evaluation in order to support his claim that the sources thesis offers a correct and explanatorily adequate account of an aspect of the law. As the analysis in Chapter 3 was intended to demonstrate, however, indirectly evaluative propositions concerning a given feature of the law do not entail any particular directly evaluative propositions regarding that feature. In claiming that issuing purportedly authoritative and binding judgements regarding what ought to be done is an important feature or function of the law which the sources thesis helps to illuminate, Raz is thus not commending this feature or function of the law as good, and nor is any such judgement entailed by his claims.

Moreover, as was also discussed in Chapter 3, a judgement that a given feature of the law is important may be justified or supported otherwise than on the basis of a direct evaluation to the effect that this same feature is good. In terms of the present discussion, this is no more than another way of rendering the point already made above that it is not necessary for legal theorists to take a stance on whether claiming to settle authoritatively certain matters by providing publicly ascertainable standards of conduct in the way which law does is a morally good thing, in order to know that the provision of such standards is an important feature of the law. Such a judgement of importance can be supported by the fact that the feature in question reveals the distinctive mode of law's operation, highlights the structure of the claims which it makes, and plays an important role in the way in which we understand and orient ourselves in our social world given the presence of law, rather than by an ascription of moral value in respect of that feature.

Another example of this kind of indirectly evaluative argument in favour of one of the tenets of Raz's theory of law can be found in the closing pages of his essay, "Authority, Law and Morality".[39] In the final section of this essay, Raz briefly attempts to defend the sources thesis from the charge that it assumes an implausible view of legislative intention. According to Raz, it follows from the fact that law necessarily claims authority that sources of law such as legislation must be under-

[39] Raz, "Authority, Law and Morality", section VI, in Raz, *Ethics in the Public Domain* (n. 20 *supra*), 235-7.

stood as expressing someone's view regarding how those subject to the law are to behave as regards the matters to which the legislation applies. This, so the objection goes, is implausible, for in the case of legislation it assumes that we can always attribute such a view to those whose task it is to make law, when we are well aware that sometimes law-makers vote while knowing little about the bill in front of them and intending only to get home as soon as they can. Raz acknowledges that there are many complexities which arise in attributing intentions to institutions rather than to individuals, and in understanding the role which such intentions play in the interpretation of the law.[40] His basic claim, however, is that we must always attribute to law-makers an intention or view about how those subject to the law are to behave, at least to the extent that we must regard their actions in voting as expressing an intent that the bill they are voting on will become law, and will be interpreted according to the conventions of interpretation of their jurisdiction.

Raz's methodological stance is revealed in the way in which he defends this claim. He argues that we are justified in regarding the actions of those who legislate in the way he describes because of the centrality to our social experience of institutions which claim to do what legislatures claim to do, i.e. to express the collective and binding judgement of society as to how members of it should behave with regard to certain matters. It is, he claims, simply part of the way in which we think about ourselves and our social world that we regard it as very important that an institution such as the United Kingdom Parliament exists and has been designed so that it can serve the function of presenting a purportedly authoritative and binding view of how people ought to behave, in the form of the legislation which emerges from it. The procedures via which a bill becomes law all testify to it being the very point of an institution like the UK Parliament that it allows the views of those who constitute it to become law: why else would those procedures make provision for Members

---

[40] See further, J. Raz, "Intention in Interpretation", in R.P. George (ed.), *The Autonomy of Law* (Oxford, Clarendon Press, 1996).

of Parliament (MPs) to debate, disagree about, seek to amend, and finally endorse or reject a certain set of proposals with a certain content, if not to allow those MPs eventually to express a collective and purportedly binding view on what ought to be done regarding those matters covered by the proposals? Given how important it is to the way we think about legal and political institutions that legislatures function so as to express a purportedly binding view on what ought to be done on certain matters, we are justified in always interpreting MPs as at least intending that the bill which they have voted in favour of will become law which will be interpreted according to the conventions of interpretation of their jurisdiction.

The fundamental point here, once again, is that in making indirectly evaluative judgements regarding the importance of certain functions which law and legal institutions are intended to serve, Raz does not seek to establish that those institutions are morally worthy or to show them in their best moral light. Rather, the point is to highlight the importance of the existence and manner of operation of certain significant social institutions, and to employ such insights in defending a particular view of certain aspects of the law. As Raz puts it:

> "in claiming that these features are important, one is not commending them as good. Their importance can be agreed upon by anarchists who reject any possibility of legitimacy for such institutions. All that is claimed is the centrality to our social experience of institutions which express what they claim to be the collective and binding judgement of their society as to how people should behave".[41]

We can close our present examination of Raz's position by briefly considering some remarks which he makes in the course of arguing against coherence-based accounts of the law.[42] Raz

[41] Raz, "Authority, Law and Morality", in Raz, *Ethics in the Public Domain* (n. 20 *supra*), 236.

[42] See J. Raz, "The Relevance of Coherence", in Raz, *Ethics in the Public Domain* (n. 20 *supra*), 277–325 for the substance of this view. Once again, my concerns here lie with Raz's remarks on the methodological presuppositions which underlie his argument, rather than with the substance of the argument itself, which I cannot explain here.

claims that the authority-based view of law which he advocates better explains its institutional nature than does the view of law as coherence, and he expands upon the nature of his argument to this effect as follows:

"while the argument, like Dworkin's, relies both on familiar and uncontroversial facts about the law and on evaluation, the evaluation concerned is not a moral one, nor is it concerned with showing American law to its best (moral) advantage. Rather, the evaluation concerns structural aspects of practical reasoning, and not its content (authority-related, content-independent justification of principles, versus their direct, content-dependent justification). The evaluation is of what is important to our understanding of the processes shaping our social environment, e.g. that the existence of social authorities is important, rather than of anything which shows them to be morally worthy".[43]

This passage provides a good summary of some of those aspects of Raz's methodological stance which I am attempting to elucidate here. One thing which is particularly important to note is the way in which that which I referred to previously as Raz's "institutional approach"[44] to understanding law informs the methodology which he adopts. For Dworkin, the focus of theorising about the law is the ascription of moral and political value to the substance of both individual laws, and to the features exhibited by law in general, in the service of trying to make the best moral sense of what the law is up to. This results in the criteria of theory-success being essentially moral criteria: for Dworkin, the best legal theory is the one which shows the content of law, whether at a greater or lesser level of abstraction, in its morally best light as an example of justified governmental coercion. For Raz, however, the criteria of success of jurisprudential theories lie not with the way in which those theories ascribe moral value to features of the law, or show them in their morally best light, but rather have to do with the ability of such theories to highlight and explain the importance of structural

---

[43] Raz, *Ethics in the Public Domain* (n. 20 *supra*), 300–1, n. 35.

[44] See the end of section A of this chapter.

features of the law which play a central role in our understanding of ourselves and of the social and political context within which a legal system operates. On this view, jurisprudential inquiry is primarily concerned not with the moral or immoral content or substance of what the law is up to, but rather with the institutional mode of law's operation: with the distinctive *way* in which it does the things it does, and the institutions via which it does them. An adequate theory of law must be able to pick out and explain which are the most important features of that mode of operation, including the institutional routes via which law operates, and the distinctive ways in which the law impinges upon and shapes our practical reasoning processes, and bears upon matters which are of practical concern to us.[45] In order to perform this task adequately, the legal theorist must of course engage in evaluation, but it is what I have referred to as indirect evaluation of the importance of certain structural features of the law and of legal institutions which are central to our self-understanding, not direct or moral evaluation or justification of those features. The interesting thing to note in the present context, then, is the way in which this distinction between indirectly evaluative judgements and directly evaluative judgements lines up with the distinction between the institutional approach to legal theory—which is concerned with highlighting the existence, structure, and mode of operation of certain important features of the law—and Dworkin's approach, which concentrates upon morally evaluating and justifying certain of those features (especially law's alleged function), in order to identify and explain the law.

To sum up the foregoing discussion: when confronted with the point that not all theories conceive of law as having the function of justifying state coercion, Dworkin tries to claim that one such theory—legal positivism—must employ an argument about law's overall point or function which is broadly similar to his own in order to be capable of providing an adequate account of the law. The above discussion tries to show that there is more to

[45] On this point, recall the discussion in Chapter 3, section B.

the jurisprudential methodological spectrum than is dreamt of in this philosophy. Razian positivism does not assume that it is the function of law to morally justify state coercion in order to draw support for various aspects of the account of law which it offers. On such an approach, indirectly evaluative judgements regarding which features of the law are the most important to explain do indeed make reference to some of the functions which we regard law as performing, but those evaluations concern the importance of those functions in understanding the social institution which exhibits them, and do not involve an assumption that law has one overall function, nor an ascription of moral value in respect of that function.[46]

Moreover, the fact that Raz's position stands strongly opposed to Dworkin's conception of law's function supports the point which I made in the last section that this conception is far from the provisional, uncontroversial and sufficiently abstract organising idea which can be assented to by all legal theorists in the name of getting them into the same interpretive ballpark. As I stated in section A, and as should by now be considerably clearer, Dworkin's view of law's function does not merely get all legal theorists into the same ballpark, but rather defines the composition, strategy and stance of one particular jurisprudential team which Dworkin, erroneously in my view, claims that everyone must be a member of if they are to have a chance of constructing a plausible legal theory. The team in question consists of those theorists who believe that: (1) it is necessary to morally evaluate the law in order to understand it; (2) that any adequate theory of law will explain how law's overall function is to police and justify state coercion; and (3) that a successful theory of law

---

[46] The interested reader might want to compare my reading of Raz's methodological stance with the far more Dworkinian reading of it offered by Stephen Perry. See e.g. S.R. Perry, "Hart's Methodological Positivism" in (1998) 4 *Legal Theory* 427, at 464; S.R. Perry, "Interpretation and Methodology in Legal Theory", in A. Marmor (ed.), *Law and Interpretation* (Oxford, Clarendon Press, 1995), at 125. Perry is of course an important contributor to this topic, and it is unfortunate that the constraints of the present project do not allow me to engage with his views directly here, save the brief remarks made in section B of Chapter 2.

will show law in its best moral light as that which justifies the use of such coercion. The discussion in this section is intended to show that those legal theorists who, like Raz, adopt an indirectly evaluative approach to legal theory, are not members of this team. They do not accept that providing a general justification for state coercion is the main aim of jurisprudential theorising, nor that it is necessary to attempt to provide such a justification in order to understand law adequately.

C. Consequences of Methodology: The Role of Legal Theory Reconsidered

The foregoing discussion attempted to illuminate the indirectly evaluative approach to legal theory from another angle, i.e. via an examination of Dworkin's view of the role which arguments about the function of law should play in successful legal theories. In so doing, this discussion sought to build upon the analysis already undertaken in earlier chapters. As I have stressed throughout this work, however, it is clear that it would require further argument to vindicate, rather than just deepen our understanding of indirectly evaluative legal theory, illustrated here by aspects of Raz's methodological stance. In part, this is because of the point raised in Chapter 1 that this work leaves largely unexplored the extent to which methodologies can be evaluated independently of the theories which rest upon them. This being the case, the book does not take a decisive stance on how far any arguments against Dworkin's methodological stance, or in favour of that espoused by Raz can take us, independently of an assessment of other aspects of the substance of their respective theories of law.

As was also noted in Chapter 1, however, no matter which view of the relation between methodologies and the theories which they support is adopted, the discussions in the book do speak to that part of the debate between legal theories which is concerned with methodology. My aim in this part of the book, then, is best characterised as being to open up the methodological presuppositions behind Dworkin's and Raz's respective

128

positions, to deepen our understanding of them, and to go some way toward exploring what those positions reveal, in terms of the possibilities for and limits of a theory of law. That project continues in this final section of the present chapter,[47] in which I briefly attempt to draw out certain of the consequences of Dworkin's approach to understanding law.

What, then, are the consequences which follow from Dworkin's distinctive take on the moral evaluation and moral justification theses, namely that in order to identify and understand the law, it is necessary to show it in its best moral light in terms of its ability to police and justify governmental collective force? One point which I want to draw attention to is that this approach results in Dworkin foreclosing the issue of whether the law is an inherently moral phenomenon more or less from the outset of his discussion, thus restricting considerably the remit of legal theoretical inquiry.

This point is, I believe, well illustrated by the analysis of Dworkin's position undertaken in previous sections of this chapter. In postulating his view of law's genre or function as the moral justification of state coercion, Dworkin assumes from the outset of the inquiry that in order to understand what law is, we must understand it as being an inherently morally justified phenomenon: law is that which sets the conditions under which state coercion is justified. The result of this is that many of those questions which it should remain open for legal theory to investigate—for example, whether law has any one overall function at all, what any such function might be, and whether that function renders law morally meritorious or justified—are closed down and answered as soon as Dworkin's point about the function of law is accepted.

The indirectly evaluative methodological approach, on the other hand, allows a legal theorist to approach the law without foreclosing at the outset questions such as whether and to what extent we must understand law to be a morally meritorious or justified phenomenon. In this type of legal theory, it is necessary to make evaluative judgements which pick out the most important

---

[47] And in the concluding chapter which follows it.

or significant features of the law to be explained, but in so doing, the legal theorist is not rendering moral judgement on those features, nor attempting to show them in their best moral and political light simply in order to identify what they are.

It might be objected, however, that I am being unfair here, on the ground that I am indicting Dworkin merely for reaching a different substantive conclusion as regards the nature of law than that which is reached by Joseph Raz, and, moreover, that I am doing so without offering sufficient argument as to why the latter's substantive theory of law is the correct one. This, however, is to miss the crux of my present concerns, which lie with the stage in Dworkin's argument at which certain jurisprudential questions are closed down. The worry here is not that Dworkin reaches the conclusion that law should be understood in its best light as the morally justified use of state coercion, but rather that his methodological stance results in this view of law being built into the very identification of the explanandum which legal philosophy seeks to investigate, from the outset. This is so because of the way in which Dworkin's point about the genre or abstract function of law defines the limits of jurisprudential inquiry from the beginning of such inquiry, namely by claiming that this view of the point or function of law sets the parameters for sensible further debate about its character. Dworkin's view of the function of law thus ensures that he comes at the law with presuppositions in place which preclude the possibility of investigating whether law has any overall function at all, or has the function of morally justifying state coercion, or is to be understood in its best moral light as that which properly constrains governmental collective force, because there is no stage in the constructive interpretation process at which these remain open questions. Rather, the point about law's genre or function assumes that all of the above is the case and builds it into the constructive interpretation process via which legal theory is to go about approaching and identifying the explanandum which it seeks to give an account of.

If it were the case, as Dworkin claims, that his view of law's genre or function is merely an abstract and provisional suggestion which does not close down the possibilities as regards future debate about the character of law, and is not a source of controversy amongst legal theorists, then he would have a way of arguing against this conclusion. He could then claim, for example, that although the task of jurisprudence is provisionally identified with the moral justification of state coercion via the construction of a political theory about law's overall point or function, that nonetheless this is open to challenge and debate. As sections A and B of the present chapter attempted to demonstrate, however, this is not the case. Dworkin's view of the function of law is not a provisional, uncontroversial and sufficiently abstract suggestion which leaves open many possibilities for debate and challenge. Rather, it is a concrete thesis about the character of law and the proper way to construct theoretical accounts of it which Dworkin regards as the only plausible option for legal theories, and which conclusively defines the stance of his particular jurisprudential team.

It is important to note that in mounting the arguments in this chapter concerning the role which Dworkin's view of the function of law plays in delimiting the task of legal theory, I still stand by my defence of his position in Chapter 5 as not falling foul of the wishful thinking objection to beneficial moral consequences arguments.[48] I am not arguing that Dworkin's view of law's function is driven by his view of which understanding of law would result in beneficial moral consequences, rather than by how law actually is. As I argued in Chapter 5, Dworkin's constructive interpretation thesis is driven not by wishful thinking, but by his view of what the social practice of law is really like, and by his stance on what we must do in order to understand practices of that kind. My concern lies rather with the way in which Dworkin goes about generating the requisite constraints on the constructive interpretation process which he claims we must undertake in order to identify and understand the kind of social practice which law is. The constructive interpretation thesis is driven by Dworkin's view of what law is like, but when

---

[48] See Chapter 5, section C.

he comes to characterise how this process is to work, he claims that the view of law's function which he postulates in order to provide the necessary constraints upon it is merely a provisional, uncontroversial and sufficiently abstract suggestion. It is this particular aspect of and stage in his argument which I seek to criticise and challenge in this chapter.

My aim in this chapter has thus been to examine Dworkin's thesis that any adequate jurisprudential theory must explain how law functions so as to provide a general justification for the exercise of state coercion. I have attempted to criticise this aspect of Dworkin's methodological stance by arguing against his claim that his view of law's function is merely a provisional, sufficiently abstract and uncontroversial organising idea. Dworkin's view of law's function is in fact doing a lot of work in his position. In setting the parameters of the kind of legal theoretical debate which Dworkin is willing to take seriously, it pins down at a very early stage in his analysis some centrally important elements in his view of what law is like. Moreover, as the analysis of Raz's work is intended to demonstrate, Dworkin's view of law's function is certainly not uncontroversial, and his insistence that all plausible legal theories, whether their authors know it or not, and despite those authors' protestations to the contrary, must have recourse to morally or directly evaluative arguments which attempt to show how law justifies state coercion, also casts doubt on his claim that his view of law's function is merely a provisional suggestion. Dworkin contends that any plausible theory of law must marshal an argument from political morality explaining why a particular view of law provides the best justification for the use of state coercion. This chapter, building upon the analysis already undertaken in Chapters 2 and 3 of the book, is intended to challenge that contention. My hope is that it has helped to explain the sense in which there is ground for an adequate theory of law to occupy—an indirectly evaluative legal theory—which does not involve making morally evaluative arguments in favour of law having a certain function, and which does not require legal theorists to understand law as providing a general justification for state coercion.

7
Carrying on the Conversation

As I stated in the introductory chapter, this work does not pretend to solve the many mysteries of jurisprudential meta-theory. Rather, it will be a success to the extent that it contributes to a better understanding of the topics with which it deals, and engenders focused debate regarding them. It is in this spirit of inviting others to carry on the conversation that the book concludes. Accordingly, my aim in this final chapter is not so much to consolidate discussions already undertaken, as to attempt to draw out some further implications of those discussions, and so point forward to avenues which might be worthy of future exploration. The remarks which follow, then, are somewhat speculative in nature, and are not intended as conclusive arguments. Rather, their purpose is to supplement the discussions in the book by signalling the direction in which my thoughts on certain issues lie.

A. The Functions of Indirectly Evaluative Legal Theory

In Chapter 2 of the book, I began my exploration of the jurisprudential methodological scene by casting aspersions on the wisdom of adhering to the descriptive/normative and value-free/value-laden dichotomies, and to the bifurcated picture of possible methodological positions which they suggest. I hope that the discussions undertaken in the book bear out my concerns in this regard. To assume that the jurisprudential methodological scene can be divided into two tribes marching under one or other of the sloganistic banners just mentioned, fails to do justice to the importance and complexity of the many issues in this area which require exploration. For example, the "two tribes" view glosses over such matters as the difference between the moral evaluation and moral justification theses and the difference between both of these and the beneficial moral consequences thesis, and may also encourage the obfuscatory myth that some approaches to legal theory—in particular legal positivism—attempt to present an account of law which is value-free.

For all this, however, there is a bifurcation of a kind involved in supporting the indirectly evaluative approach to legal theory which has been discussed in this work, in that this approach is committed to there being a distinction between the enterprise which addresses questions such as "what is law/what is the special character of this type of social institution?", on the one hand, and that which addresses questions such as "which norms ought to be obeyed?", "which values ought a legal system to live up to?", and "under which conditions are legal systems justified?", on the other. In keeping with the terminology introduced in this work, we could say that attempting to answer the first set of questions requires recourse to indirect evaluation in order to identify which are the important and significant features of the law to be explained, whereas the second set of issues involves asking and attempting to answer directly evaluative questions in respect of whether those features and the social institution which exhibits them are good or bad, justified or unjustified, etc. For shorthand purposes, I sometimes refer to these as the indirectly evaluative and the directly evaluative enterprise respectively.

However, although the indirectly evaluative legal theorist holds that these two enterprises or sets of questions can be separated, and that we can and should try to answer the first set prior to and relatively independently of the second, still it should not be thought that the enterprises or sets of questions are, for this reason, entirely unconnected, or that pursuing the first in a certain manner cannot advance the pursuit of the second. Recall that whilst elucidating the distinction between directly evaluative and indirectly evaluative propositions in Chapter 3, I also postulated a possible link between them, to the effect that indirectly evaluative propositions could sometimes be supported by the

134

fact that the features of the law which they pick out as important to explain are relevant to answering directly evaluative questions such as whether and under what conditions law is a good or morally justified phenomenon.[1] That is to say, I suggested that one reason why certain features of the law *are* important to explain is because an understanding of them is vital if we are to be able to directly evaluate the law, or, to put it in a slightly different way, to subject the law to moral scrutiny. This link also has significance in the present context, for it assists in explaining the way in which the first, indirectly evaluative enterprise in legal theory is related to the second, directly evaluative one, whilst still retaining relative independence from it.

That aspect of the relation between these enterprises which I wish to highlight here trades on the thought that in order to directly evaluate whether a social institution such as law is good or bad, and to make a judgement on what we ought to do with regard to it, we must first of all know quite a lot about the features of it which are relevant to such an evaluation. If we are to be capable of answering directly evaluative questions such as whether and under what conditions legal norms ought to be obeyed, then we need to know quite a bit about how those norms, and the social institution which issues them, operate. Otherwise, how are we to know *what* exactly we are asking the question, "ought we to obey it?" of? In asking whether we ought to obey the law, we are asking whether we ought to obey a particular sort of social institution which differs from other forms of social organisation in that it operates via certain distinctive procedures and institutional means. We need to know, therefore, what those procedures and means are in order to have the information relevant to trying to answer whether law ought to be obeyed. In fact, we need to know quite a lot about the nature of the institutions and procedures via which law operates even to be able to *ask* the directly evaluative questions about it which we wish to, for, at least in some cases, we cannot even formulate those questions with any degree of precision or accuracy until

[1] See Chapter 3, section B.

we know quite a bit about the distinctive character of law. For example, if we are going to ask and attempt to answer the question of whether and under what conditions the law's claim that it possesses moral authority and creates reasons for action for those subject to it which they would not otherwise have is true,[2] we first of all need to know that the law is a particular sort of social institution which, amongst other things, always makes claims to authority over those subject to it which have a certain structure, namely that they purport to create reasons for action of a certain kind which they would not otherwise have. This is already a lot to identify and explain about the nature of law. There are, therefore, many prior questions which we need to ask and attempt to answer before we can even get to the point where we can formulate, let alone answer, the directly evaluative questions about the law which we might eventually wish to.

Investigating those prior questions which reveal the nature of law, and which tell us what is distinctive about this social institution, and how it differs from other forms of social organisation, is the task of indirectly evaluative legal theory. As was suggested in Chapter 3, this indirectly evaluative enterprise can be viewed as being tied to the one which attempts to answer directly evaluative questions, because sometimes the reason why it is important to understand a particular feature of the law is that this understanding will be relevant to eventually answering directly evaluative questions such as whether and under what circumstances the law is a good or a bad thing, and hence whether and under what circumstances we should obey it. In light of the remarks above, if we now consider this point from, as it were, the other side, from the point of view of the directly evaluative enterprise as opposed to the indirectly evaluative

---

[2] This, roughly speaking, is the question which Stephen Perry takes as the central question of jurisprudence, see S.R. Perry, "Is a Descriptive Theory of Law Possible?" (manuscript, New York, 2000), and also S.R. Perry, "Hart's Methodological Positivism" in (1998) 4 *Legal Theory* 427, especially section VII. My thinking on these issues was aided by the discussion of Perry's paper, "Is a Descriptive Theory of Law Possible?" (*ibid.*) at a workshop on meta-legal theory held in Columbia University Law School, New York on 24 and 25 March 2000.

enterprise, then another way of viewing this link between them emerges. From the perspective of the directly evaluative enterprise, one function of an indirectly evaluative judgement to the effect that a given feature of law is important is that it can perform the necessary task of homing in on and explaining the nature of those features of the law which would be relevant to any eventual direct evaluation of it.

In other words, it is not merely the case that those engaging in indirectly evaluative legal theory can pick out which features of the law are important to explain—including features which would be relevant to its eventual direct or moral evaluation—without returning directly evaluative judgements regarding whether those features, and the social institution which exhibits them, are good or bad, justified or unjustified. Rather, the point to be grasped is that one function of such judgements of importance is that they can identify and analyse those features of the law which are relevant to its eventual direct evaluation, or to subjecting the law to moral scrutiny. An indirectly evaluative judgement of the importance of a given feature of law can thus identify that feature as something which it would be relevant to consider in any eventual direct evaluation of whether the institution is good or bad, but does not itself perform or entail such an evaluation. In this way, then, in constructing successful indirectly evaluative legal theories, we are undertaking a necessary first step on the road to answering some of the directly evaluative questions which we might want to ask of the law.

Moreover, although the indirectly evaluative approach to legal theory does not return directly evaluative judgements upon, for example, the law's claim to possess legitimate authority and to create reasons for actions for those subject to it which it picks out as important to explain, understanding what claims like these consist in is vitally important if we are to go on to directly evaluate them and the social institution which makes them. By this I mean that, at least in part, it is what the law claims to be, and the ideals which it claims to live up to, which set the standard by which it is to be assessed when we go on to make directly evaluative judgements about it.

The reason for this is that it is important to know what sort of thing something is trying to be before we settle upon the standards by which it ought to be judged. Consider the case of an electric toaster and a toy electric toaster. If something is supposed to be a toy electric toaster, then we will hold it to very different standards than if it is supposed to be a real electric toaster.[3] Similarly, with the law, it is important to know what kind of thing it aspires to be before we decide which standards it should be judged by. It seems very plausible that those standards are, at least in part, set by the kind of thing which law reveals itself as aspiring to be in the claims which it makes. That is to say, if the law claims moral authority, and to create reasons for action of a certain kind which we would not otherwise have, then whether it truly does possess such authority, and does create such reasons for action, would seem to be important standards to which we should hold law in assessing whether it is good or not. This being the case, in picking out those characteristic claims of law which it is important to explain, an indirect evaluation of them makes available to us some of the standards by which law should be directly evaluated.

Mentioning this point raises more questions than can be settled here. For example, in light of it, we might wish to consider whether a social institution such as law should ever be judged by standards which it does not itself claim to aspire to, and whether and to what extent the distinctive nature of law renders its self-proclaimed ideals particularly important to its evaluation. These are questions which cannot be addressed here, although I regard them as interesting matters which are worthy of future investigation.

The foregoing remarks reveal a little more about my view of the relation between the indirectly evaluative and directly evaluative enterprises. What if the objection were to be raised, however, that in advertising itself as allowing us to get a clear view of certain features of the social institution of law before we go on to offer a direct or moral evaluation of it, the indirectly evaluative approach to legal theory leaves itself open to the kind of

---

[3] Thanks are due to Catherine Holmes and Jeyanthi John for this example.

charge which I pressed against Frederick Schauer in Chapter 5.[4] Do the suggestions made above not also involve arguing in what I claimed is the wrong direction: *from* the beneficial consequences which would ensue *if* we can separate the indirectly evaluative from the directly evaluative enterprise (namely that we will be able to gain a clear view of the social institution of law, before we go on to evaluate whether or not it is a good thing/whether or not we ought to obey it) *to* the conclusion that therefore we can separate the indirectly evaluative from the directly evaluative enterprise?[5]

This question takes us right to very limits of the present work, and, in particular, to the limitation imposed upon the discussions in it by the point mentioned in Chapter 1 that it seems unlikely in the case of legal theory that methodologies can be conclusively evaluated independently of the substantive accounts of law which rest upon them, and independently of assessing, for example, how well those substantive accounts gel with our common, pre-theoretical understanding of the law. This being so, although I believe that the above objection can be rebutted, this can only be fully achieved by pointing to the nature of law itself, which is such that we can and should identify and explain the essential properties of this social institution without returning directly evaluative judgements upon them.

In other words, the foregoing remarks concerning the relation between the indirectly evaluative and directly evaluative enterprises do not constitute an illegitimate argument from the beneficial consequences of adopting a certain approach to understanding the law to the correctness of that approach. Rather, they seek to elucidate what follows from the thesis that the proper way to go about understanding law's essential properties *is* via indirectly evaluative legal theory. Conclusively establishing this thesis, however, is dependent to some extent upon an argument about the law itself, to the effect that the nature of

[4] See Chapter 5, section A.

[5] Schauer's argument, of course, concerned the merits of the social thesis rather than of indirectly evaluative legal theory. My question is merely whether the same *kind* of problem may be inherent in both arguments.

law dictates that the correct way to go about understanding it is via the indirectly evaluative methodological approach. As I certainly cannot develop or defend a full-blown account of the nature of law here, this cannot be conclusively established. In the remainder of this section, then, I attempt merely to sketch out certain important features in my view of what law is like, and to draw attention to the significance of those features for the thesis that the indirectly evaluative methodological approach is the correct one for a legal theory to adopt.

As I already discussed in Chapter 2, the concept of law—unlike some of the concepts which feature in, for example, theoretical physics or some branches of criminology—is one with which members of our society are very familiar.[6] Irrespective of whether they have ever heard of legal *theory*, those living in a society governed by law are usually aware of the law's existence and of certain features of it; for instance, that it claims to tell us what to do in respect of some areas of our conduct, that it considers itself to be obligatory, and that it operates via special sorts of institutions and institutional means: the courts, lawyers, policemen, purportedly authoritative governmental edicts, etc. As has also been argued throughout this work, it is these familiar features of law, and the way that they are thought of by those living under the law, which are important to explain. Moreover, in my view, it is this aspect of the nature of the data with which legal theory is concerned which mitigates strongly in favour of the thesis that the indirectly evaluative methodological approach is the correct one for a legal theory to adopt.

My contention, then, is simply this: when we approach a given society and want to know whether it is regulated by law, we need not attempt to work out which norms will be rightly treated as morally obligatory by the truly practically reasonable man, and nor need we construct a comprehensive political theory which puts the past and present edicts of the government of that society in their morally best light. The reason for this is that we already find ourselves faced with a richness of obvious

[6] See Chapter 2, section C.

data, in the form of courts and other legal institutions and officials, and a whole host of purportedly binding legal norms which the subjects of that society are aware of and make use of in their daily lives in organising their affairs and in reasoning about what to do. Irrespective of the moral or other goodness of those norms, and of the moral or other goodness of the distinctive institutions and procedures from which they emanate, the law impinges upon the lives of those living under it, and does so in certain distinctive ways which mark it out as the kind of social institution which it is. That law has these effects, and that it has them owing to the distinctive way in which it operates, and irrespective of the moral or immoral substance of what it is up to, is a fundamental feature of the law, and of the way that we think about and orient ourselves with regard to it. We are all aware that where a legal system is in existence we will find special sorts of institutions and procedures, and we are also aware that the law will operate via those institutions and procedures—to the extent of removing our freedom if we disobey it—whether we are in moral agreement with it or not, and whether it is functioning so as properly to police and justify state coercion or not.

My claim, then, is simply that it is part of our common understanding of the law that wherever a legal system is in existence it operates via distinctive institutions and procedures, and that it does so regardless of whether what issues from those institutions is an instance of morally justified state coercion or is promulgated for the common good. As was discussed in Chapter 2, a successful legal theory must adequately reflect and explain the way in which those subject to the law think about and understand it. Whether or not we wish to go on to morally evaluate the law, or to test whether and under what conditions it morally justifies state coercion, the existence of powerful sorts of social institutions which we regard as being different from other forms of social organisation and which operate in distinct ways—sometimes to the right ends, and sometimes to the wrong ends—is just something which is fundamental to the way in which we think about law and which is thus vitally important to explain.

It should be noted that these brief remarks are not intended to suggest that it is the job of legal theory merely to report upon beliefs about the law held by those subject to it, and so to present a kind of opinion poll as regards who thinks what about the nature of law. As has already been mentioned in the course of a previous discussion, analytical jurisprudence does much more than merely report on views about the law held by those subject to it, and those views themselves are not held in anything like the form in which they appear in jurisprudential writings.[7] For all that, however, the point remains that jurisprudence has a responsibility to systematise and explain the way that we think about law and the distinctions which we draw and refuse to draw in respect of the operation of this social institution. That we regard there as being something important and distinctive about forms of social organisation which we hold to be legal systems, and that we regard those forms of social organisation as always operating via distinctive institutional routes and procedures, irrespective of the moral or immoral substance of what they are up to on particular occasions is simply part of the data which legal theory has a duty to illuminate and help us better understand.

It is these distinctive features of legal regulation and of the way in which we think about law which indirectly evaluative legal theory picks out as important and significant to explain. Owing to the nature of the data with which legal theory is concerned, it is possible to identify legal phenomena, and to pick out which features of the legal system are the most important to explain, without delving into directly evaluative questions regarding when and under what conditions such a system is morally justified. Once we have dealt with and explained the nature of those distinctive institutions and procedures which we account as legal, we will then be in a position to go on to consider whether those institutions and procedures are, for example, capable of morally justifying state coercion, or create reasons for action for those subject to the law which they would not otherwise have. I am not denying the importance of such

[7] See p. 43 *supra*.

questions, but rather merely pointing out that before attempting to answer them, we should try first of all to gain knowledge and understanding of what it is that we are asking them of.

To sum up: the nature of the phenomena under consideration, and of the way in which we commonly think about it, is what drives the indirectly evaluative approach to understanding the law. The wisdom of adopting such an indirectly evaluative account is to be judged not in terms of our wishful thinking about the best way to understand law, but rather is subject to the criterion of success that it can best systematise and explain certain elements in our common conception of what law is like. I thus believe that the claims made on behalf of indirectly evaluative legal theory in this chapter can be defended from the type of charge which I levelled at Schauer in Chapter 5. In suggesting that the indirectly and directly evaluative enterprises, although relatively independent, are not entirely unconnected, and that the first enterprise, properly conducted, can advance the second, I am not arguing from that consequence to the proper nature of legal theoretical understanding, but rather merely seeking to draw out certain implications of the point that the proper way to go about understanding law's essential properties *is* via an indirectly evaluative theory of law. Considering those implications assists in explaining the sense in which, although relatively independent from each other, the indirectly evaluative and the directly evaluative enterprise can be mutually enhancing activities.

Indirectly evaluative legal theory can thus be viewed as serving a dual function. In the first instance, this methodological approach seeks to deepen our understanding of a centrally important social institution which has a pervasive influence on the lives of those living under it. It should be noted that I regard this task as being extremely valuable in its own right, whether or not the theorist concerned wishes to go on to directly or morally evaluate that which his theory of law has explained. However, indirectly evaluative legal theory can also help us to pick out and understand those facets of legal regulation which will be important to the eventual direct or moral evaluation of the law. In so doing, it can operate as an illuminating precursor to important

143

tasks such as considering the moral value of the law, subjecting law to critical moral scrutiny, and deciding whether and under what circumstances we ought to obey it.

B. Conclusion

In this work, I have attempted to deepen our understanding of some important issues in jurisprudential methodology, and to locate the views of some major legal theorists with respect to them. My main aim has been to illuminate the nature of an approach to legal theory, indirectly evaluative legal theory, which I believe has not been well understood to date, and to defend that approach from some of the criticisms which have been levelled at it. The book began with a question: what's the point of jurisprudence? My basic answer to it remains unmodified from my starting point in chapter one, i.e. that an analytical jurisprudential theory seeks to explain the nature of law by attempting to identify and provide an account of its essential properties. I hope, however, that the discussions in the book have gone some way towards fleshing out my view of how we are to go about achieving that aim, and what will be the point in so doing.

So—how *are* we to go about explaining the nature of law? By rejecting the moral evaluation, moral justification and beneficial moral consequences theses, and adopting the indirectly evaluative approach to legal theory which seeks to pick out and explain the important and significant features of law, without prejudging the issue of whether or not they render law a good or justified phenomenon. What will be the point in so doing? To deepen our understanding of a centrally important social institution which has a pervasive influence on our lives, and to serve as an illuminating precursor to the enterprise of assessing whether, in what sense, and under what conditions the law may be morally worthy.

These brief concluding comments bring my present contribution to this jurisprudential inquiry to a close. The lines remain open, however, and I very much hope that others will respond to the ideas expressed here and so carry on the conversation.

Index

Index

Index